THE COURTHOUSE
AT EDENTON

THE COURTHOUSE AT EDENTON

A HISTORY OF THE CHOWAN COUNTY COURTHOUSE OF 1767

MARC D. BRODSKY

PUBLISHED BY CHOWAN COUNTY
EDENTON, NORTH CAROLINA

Published in 1989 by Chowan County, Edenton, North Carolina

Library of Congress Catalog Card Number: 89-60832
Cloth Binding ISBN 0-9622742-0-8
Paperbound ISBN 0-9622742-1-6

Brodsky, Marc D., 1955–
    The courthouse at Edenton: a history of the Chowan County
        courthouse of 1767 / Marc D. Brodsky.
        p. cm.
    Includes bibliographical references.
    ISBN 0-9622742-0-8   ISBN 0-9622742-1-6 (pbk.)
    1. Chowan County Courthouse (Edenton, N.C.)   2. Edenton (N.C.)
— Buildings, structures, etc.   3. Edenton (N.C.) — History.   I. Title.
F264.E3B76   1989
975.6'147—dc20   89-60832
                                                              CIP

All proceeds from the sale of this book will contribute to the restoration and maintenance of the Chowan County Courthouse in Edenton, North Carolina.

Book Design and Production: Robert L. Bryden, Chapel Hill, North Carolina. **Photography**: Seth Tice-Lewis, Chapel Hill, North Carolina. **Typography**: Liberated Types, Ltd., Durham, North Carolina. **Printing**: Ferguson Printing Company, Durham, North Carolina.

Cover Photograph: CHOWAN COUNTY COURTHOUSE, 2 APRIL 1890. Note the absence of the clock in the cupola. (North Carolina Collection, University of North Carolina Library at Chapel Hill)

Contents

CHOWAN COUNTY COURTHOUSE;
EDENTON, NORTH CAROLINA

Introduction:
The Courthouse at Edenton

This book presents a history of the Old Chowan County Courthouse in Edenton, North Carolina. The results of research directed towards the building's structural history, including descriptions of alterations, additions, and repairs to both the interior and exterior of the building will form the core of this text.

Overall, a broader view of the courthouse will be considered, one which examines the links between the courthouse and the community it has served since 1767; the place of the courthouse as one of a group of judicial, legislative, and community buildings that have occupied portions of the same public lots in Edenton since before 1720; and thus the position of the courthouse within a larger historical landscape. Very often basic questions regarding the function of the courthouse (or another building) may relate not only to 'improvements' made on the building, but also to the economic life of the area. For example, the decision to 'zinck' the courthouse roof, originally made in June 1833, refers to the special needs of a building that must protect important documents from fire. It also leads to the unacceptable job done by the contracting company, Edenton's Houghton and Booth, to the collapse of that company, the effect upon Edenton of that collapse, and finally to a new shingle roof on the courthouse.

The courthouse is also to be regarded as a superb building, appropriate to a town which was a leading commercial as well as judicial center of activity. Routinely called 'perhaps the finest Georgian Courthouse in the South', it is, as a building far from routine. Displaying classic Georgian line, proportion and detail, set impressively at the end of a long rectangular green overlooking the Bay, the Chowan County Courthouse is an exceptional example of colonial architecture. The two story brick building features a five bay symmetrical facade which includes a central, slightly projecting pedimented pavillion. The walls are laid in Flemish bond over a water table of stouter and stronger English bond. The foundation is made of brick as are the interior walls which divide the central portion of the building from the offices on either side of it. These walls also encompass the two chimneys which face each other across the central space which contains the courtroom and the upper Assembly Room. The main entry way is flanked on the outside by a pair of pilasters, and opens directly through double hung panelled doors into the courtroom. There is no waiting area or entry hall. These doors originally opened into the building, rather than pulling out as they do now. Passage to the second story is conducted by way of a stair hall. The upstairs Assembly Room measures thirty-three feet by forty-five feet and is fully panelled. The panelling includes a molded chairrail, and is topped by a full entablature with a dentilled cornice. There are breaks or slight projections in the panelling above each door or window in the room. The sash windows of the lower floor are nine feet tall, and are arranged in a pattern of nine over nine. The slightly smaller windows of the second story are placed in a nine over six pattern. Segmented arches of fine gauged work of rubbed brick highlight and crown each of the windows. In Georgian style, the horizontal lines of the building representing the division of the two stories are emphasized by the water table, a central string course, and in this case, a modillioned cornice. The vertical line of the courthouse in which the central pavillion participates is begun by the pedimented entrance and doorway, enhanced by the line of the hipped roof, and culminates in the cupola/clock tower. The lower stage of the cupola carries its own open pediment and bracket which protect the foward and two side clockfaces. In each face of the cupola's upper octagonal stage is a tall slender arched window opening. Finally, a spire and weather vane stand atop the uppermost roof. This quick tour identifies many of the architectural features which attest to the care, skill, and expense that went into the design and construction of this building. The Chowan County Courthouse may be described in its own way as simple, functional, and elegant. It also reflects a long living history, and is the bearer of tradition.

The building at the center of this investigation is also a meeting ground of individuals and historical forces. Men and women of service and stature spoke and worked here, some with familiar 'historically significant' names, others less well known except to those folks who live in and around Chowan County. In the 1770's, Edenton could claim among its citizens Joseph Hewes, a signer of the Declaration of Independence; Samuel Johnston, who would become the first Senator from the State of North Carolina; and James Iredell,

PANELLED ASSEMBLY HALL ON THE
SECOND FLOOR OF THE COURTHOUSE

FRONT STEPS OF THE COURTHOUSE

who would later be appointed by George Washington to the United States Supreme Court. All three of these men were active in various capacities as officers of the County Court. Their presence along with that of Hugh Williamson, a signer of the United States Constitution and a physician who had moved to Edenton in 1777, contributed to Edenton's status as an intellectual center of revolutionary resistance against the British, and of active concern and participation in the formation and development of the new nation. Discussions regarding help for a blockaded and beleagured Boston, ratification of a national constitution, and secession from the union were held at the courthouse, as were church meetings of all kinds, benefits for local organizations, exhibitions of the academic achievement of young students, and over 175 years of meetings by the local Masons. A President of the United States was entertained here, Negro slaves were commonly 'divided' as part of the settlement of estates. Men and women were whipped nearby as punishment for crimes. As technologies changed, so did the heating, lighting, and plumbing at the courthouse. The daily business of the Register of Deeds and Clerk of Court always took place. The courthouse will be considered as an historical site, a particular building at any one particular moment in time, and as a structure which has participated in the matrix of history. It is hoped that a balance between the more strictly architectural and the historical will be served throughout.

The course of the book will proceed in the following manner. The first chapter will examine the origins and predecessors of the 1767 courthouse. This is meant to situate the courthouse within both a legislative history, beginning with the 1712 Act of Assembly which established the town at Queen Anne's Creek, and within that group of public buildings which first defined the center of Edenton; the first Chowan Courthouse, the Council Chamber, the early County jails, and the warehouses which stood towards the foot of what is now the Courthouse Green. The focus of attention will be on these buildings, their locations, and to the status and description of Edenton in general.

The next five chapters will detail and document the history of the 1767 courthouse. Significant areas of the building will be examined for each of several periods of time. These periods will be largely determined by the life of the building itself, that is, by the schedule of changes undergone. As one might expect, this 'schedule and life' will itself have been influenced by political events and social conditions. Upon reaching a point roughly half-way through the history of the building, a brief consideration of Edenton as it moved through the mid to late nineteenth century will be offered. The view of the courthouse will continue up through the transition made in 1979-80 when the third Chowan County Courthouse assumed primary responsibility for court and county matters.

Each of these periods of time will also include, under a separate heading, information regarding the County jail and selected other public structures of interest in Edenton. As the two primary county buildings in Edenton, the courthouse and jail were often paired together when it came time to assess the condition of county buildings and to repair deficiencies. The two buildings are also linked in other ways. Besides sharing in the function of administering justice, they also stand in close proximity to each other on the same pair of town lots. The jailer, who often doubled as courthouse keeper lived for many years in the house which is flanked immediately by both buildings. Also, newly uncovered information having to do with several Chowan County jails will be presented. As for the other buildings and structures to be mentioned in this report, all can be grouped together along with the courthouse and jail as part of the complex of public buildings in Edenton.

Among the most important sources used in preparing this history were the Minutes of the County Court of Pleas and Quarter Sessions. The Court, whose functions remained largely unchanged from the colonial period, through the Revolution, and into the nineteenth century had among its duties the care and maintenance of county buildings, including the courthouse. With North Carolina's adoption of a new State Constitution in 1868, the Court's judicial and administrative functions were reassigned, and a newly created Board of County Commissioners was given responsibility for the public buildings. The Minutes from the meetings of this Board provided much information regarding the courthouse for the years 1868 to the present time, just as the Court Minutes did for the years prior to that date. These primary records from Chowan County are virtually continuous and intact back to the 1740's. No major fires were reported at the courthouse. None of these records were lost due to storm related damage or the intrusion of war. This in itself is an extraordinary fact. Other county records including the papers of prominent Edenton and Chowan County residents, as well as newspapers of the time were among the documents which were also used extensively.

In addition to presenting an informative and factual account of the courthouse and its place in Edenton, this inquiry will pose important questions which continue to go unanswered. For example, the major mysteries concerning the courthouse, the identity of its designer and builder, and the financial details surrounding its construction, persist. Unfortunately, no documentation was found which allows any statement beyond speculation and suggestion on these questions. Pertinent material which may inform and add to this speculation will be presented and considered.

Finally, it is hoped that the various perspectives employed here will be of use and interest to different people for various purposes, that the architectural historian, inquisitive visitor, restoration specialist, and interested citizen of Chowan County might all add to their knowedge and appreciation of the estimable Chowan County Courthouse.

VIEW TOWARDS THE BAY FROM AN
ASSEMBLY HALL WINDOW

From the Beginning:
Edenton and its Buildings
1712-1766

Present day Edenton had its official beginning in the eyes of the colonial government with the passage of an Act of Assembly in November 1712. Listed among the Laws of North Carolina in 1715, the Act was "to promote the building of a Court House to hold the Assembly in, at the fork of Queen Anne's Creek, commonly called Matchacamak Creek in Chowan Precinct."[1] The making of the town (still referred to by location, not by any name), the fixing of the location of the Assembly, and the legislation which encouraged the building of a courthouse were one and the same act. The land upon which the town was to be established was offered by Nathaniel Chevin and Thomas Peterson. Chevin's land was a 100 acre tract at the fork of Queen Anne's Creek which had formerly been granted to John Porter of London. On 22 May 1707 as a result of Porter's death, his grant having lapsed, the 100 acres reverted back to the government. Chevin then received his own patent for the land which was duly, if belatedly, registered on 25 March 1712.[2] The Act passed in November of that year authorized this land to be divided into one half acre lots, each to be sold for 20 shillings. Two acres were to be set aside and assigned for a courthouse, a church, and other public uses. This was the start of the town at Queen Anne's Creek.

Peterson's land consisted of 270 acres which joined Chevin's. Although this tract was not bought or included within the limits of the town until Edenton was incorporated under that name in 1722[3] (well after Peterson's death in 1715), both Peterson and Chevin were installed as trustees empowered to divide the original 100 acres and to assign and transfer the lots of one half acre each. The requirement for keeping any of these lots was to build upon them a habitable dwelling of not less than 15 x 20 feet within one year. On 1 September 1715 the first of these lots, designated by the letter "A", went to Charles Fortce.[4] By 1720 both Chevin and Peterson were dead and the majority of the 100 acres had neither been allotted nor laid out. In another Act passed by the Assembly in that year, responsibility for completing the task was vested in Daniel Richardson.[5] Richardson, Receiver General of the colony since 4 April 1713,[6] was charged with reserving places in town for sufficient streets, a burying place, and a market, in addition to the two acres which were already set aside for public uses. With the incorporation of Edenton in 1722, 140 of Peterson's 270 acres were ordered marked off into half acre lots. The remainder were to be held in common for the people of the town. Joanna Peterson, Thomas' widow, was to be paid £300 for the land and the improvements upon it. Christopher Gale, one of the newly appointed Commissioners of the town was named Treasurer and Receiver of all money arising from the sale of these lots. Edenton grew once more in these early years, reaching a size of 420 acres, when on 11 August 1723 Robert Hicks deeded to the Commissioners one half of a 100 acre tract which bordered on the back of the town.[7]

From a reading of the Acts of Assembly regarding the establishment, growth, and regulation of Queen Anne's Town/Edenton, several things are clear. First, the setting aside of land for a church, courthouse, and other public buildings was part of the earliest plan of the town. For this reason there are no deeds for these original plots. Second, with the fixing of the location of the Assembly at the courthouse in 1712, and the later provision in 1722 for the building of a Governor's House and a Council Room, Queen Anne's Town was certainly formed, and Edenton incorporated as the seat of North Carolina government. It may be noted that contingent upon the construction of that Council Room and a jail, the Act also required the Chief Justice, Secretary, Attorney General, Surveyor General, and several other ranking public officials to keep their offices in Edenton.[8] Also, regarding this same matter, on two occasions in the text of an Act passed in 1723 having to do with various matters relating to several towns, Edenton is described as "Metropolis" of the government, meaning its capital.[9]

The courthouse was the first of these public buildings to be constructed. Records show that the first use of this courthouse occurred on 31 July 1716. On that date, "a General Court or Court of Pleas and Court of Oyer and Terminer and General Gaol Delivery [was] held at the Court House Queen Anne's Creek." The Justices present were Christopher Gale, Chief Justice; and his assistants Griffin Jones, John Palin, and Thomas Harvey.[10] Although this is the first time that the courthouse is mentioned, the records show that as soon as the court was called to order, it was adjourned to meet later that day at William Branch's house.[11] The next session, convened in August 1716, also met at his house.[12] Not far from the public lots, Branch lived on fifty acres purchased from Jon. Davis on 4 July 1704 at the head and on the south side of Queen Anne's Creek.[13] In fact, the next five sessions of court either

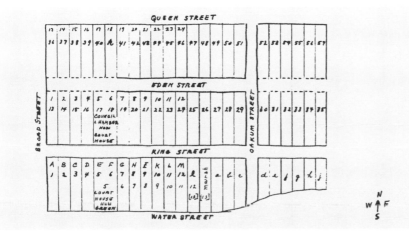

EDENTON TOWN LOTS, OLD PLAN. All lots east of Broad Street are called Old Plan lots; those west of it, New Plan. Capital letters and numbers at top of lots used through 1725. Numbers in second row used as early as 1714, with lower case letters for low-lying or incomplete lots. Numbers in third row (waterfront lots) as early as 1725. (Drawing by Elizabeth Moore, reprinted, by permission from Hoffman, *Chowan Precinct, N.C. 1693-1723, Genealogical Abstracts of Deed Books.*)

CHRISTOPHER GALE. Colonial Chief Justice of North Carolina, Gale presided over the first session of Court "held at the Courthouse Queen Anne's Creek" in 1716. Along with the names of several of Edenton's judges, Gale is honored on a commemorative tablet which hangs in the courtroom of the Chowan County Courthouse. (North Carolina Division of Archives and History, Raleigh, North Carolina)

met at Branch's house, or opened 'at the Court House' only to be immediately adjourned to reconvene there.[14] It was not until 29 July 1718 that an entire session of court was held and completed at the courthouse at Queen Anne's Creek.[15] As for the intervening two years, we may only assume that the site of the courthouse, though already designated, was not yet ready to serve the needs of the court. Interestingly enough, William Branch's will shows that he also owned a house on the Edenton lot identified as 'B', just west of the courthouse lot. He did, however, not acquire this land until 27 July 1718, just about the same time the courthouse is recorded as having become fully usable.[16]

Prior to this period, it was the usual practice to hold the several courts of the colony; General, Precinct, and Chancery, (these were the most common), at private homes. From 1709 until 1715 the General Court met almost exclusively at John Hecklefield's house in Little River (in what is now Perquimans County), an exception being a session held at Thomas Lee's house in Chowan. Later meetings were held at the house of Richard Sanderson, also of Little River, and as we have seen, at William Branch's house.[17] Precinct courts also met at Branch's, and on at least one occasion at Robert Hicks'.[18] The Court of Chancery, consisting of the Governor and the Council usually met at the governor's house, or in his absence, at that of the court's presiding officer. From August 1712 to April 1719 Edward Hyde, Thomas Pollock, Thomas Lee, Frederick Jones, William Dukenfield, and Richard Sanderson all held court at their homes. After 1719, the court was moved to an unspecified location in town, presumably until the Council Chamber was built.[19] On 11 November 1718, the Executive Council held its first meeting at the courthouse. At that meeting, the courthouse was also selected as the site of the next General Assembly, to be held the following March.[20]

The first "Chowan County Courthouse" was a wooden frame building roofed with shingles and plastered on the inside. The account of the expenditure for the building shows a total cost of £287..17..9. Edward Moseley acted as Commissioner or Treasurer of the project. He drew up the account which is dated 9 March 1719.[21] More than half of the sum was paid to Capt. Lee (perhaps Thomas Lee, mentioned above) who supplied the plank among other materials and services. Others paid for the construction were Capt. Fortce, listed as/for a carpenter; Mr. Bray, for nails; John Marks, for shingles; Mr. Paine, for oyster shells and plastering; and Mr. Vail, also for nails. These are the only materials and costs mentioned. Other material which may have been used is simply not shown on the account. Glass windows, for example, in place at the courthouse by the 1750's appear not to have been part of the original construction. They may have been included in the building from the start, or, more probably, added later. Window openings with wooden shutters may have been used until the glass was installed. This is the building described by William Byrd upon his visit to Edenton in 1728 when he said, "Justice herself is but indifferently Lodged, the courthouse having much the air of a Common Tobacco-House."[22]

Even before Byrd's visit, the General Assembly seems to have been less than satisfied with this first courthouse. On 2 October 1722 an Act was passed providing for a new courthouse, no smaller than 24 by 16 feet, for

Chowan Precinct.[23] On 3 May 1723 the Commissioners of Edenton sold lots 58 and 59 of the old plan (East of Broad Street) to the Justices of Chowan Precinct for the purpose of building a courthouse.[24] This courthouse was never built. In 1736 the lots were resold to John Richards, the title of the Justices, "having lapsed for want of a building."[25]

At about the same time the Justices were buying land for a new courthouse, the Council Chamber or Room, also authorized by the Assembly, was built. It is possible that when faced with the prospect of building this structure (and a jail), Edenton's Commissioners decided to maintain the existing court-house and to go ahead with the other much needed construction. The Council Chamber was begun sometime after 19 October 1722[26] and was occupied by 17 April 1724. It is curious to note that whereas the Council Minutes place this April session simply "in Edenton", an order from that session is dated and closed from "the Council Chamber in Edenton".[27] Since several of the preceeding council meetings are also placed "in Edenton", it is difficult to say exactly when the Chamber was first used. The next session of the Council occurred in July 1724 and clearly took place at the Council Chamber.[28] According to Paschal, the new structure was to be used by the Council and the Assembly, in addition to housing the offices of the agencies of government as outlined in the Act which incorporated Edenton. When the Council met as the upper house of the General Assembly, it would sit at the Council Chamber, while the lower house would meet at the courthouse.[29]

Very little is known about the Council Chamber itself. Motions were made in July and August 1740 by the Council to have James Craven repair the Chamber at a cost not exceeding £100.[30] Unfortunately, no details regarding this situation are available. References among the Chowan County papers to repair work on the building do not occur until the 1750's. But even these clues only reveal a frame building with a brick chimney and several windows. From an account with Thomas Barker for work done in 1758 by Gilbert Leigh, a house carpenter and joiner, we find a large number of lights of glass being replaced, forty-five; a charge for Leigh's labor, and for that of William Frasier. Other charges for nails, a bucket of white wash, finding plank, and laying the "harth" were also recorded. The bill totaled £7..5..0.[31] Leigh again repaired the chamber, presenting an account for £4..5..5 proclamation money to the July 1760 session of court.[32] A final reference appears on an account with Sheriff William Halsey from May 1763 which lists an expendi-ture of £2..5..0 going towards mending the Council Room.[33]

The origins of the jail for the Precinct of Chowan are also unclear. As was the case with the Council Chamber, we know that a jail was planned for Edenton by the time the town was incorporated in 1722. References to a Public Gaol specifically in Edenton occur in the Colonial Records by 9 April 1726.[34] Other information about the origins of this structure or about any other jails prior to 1722 in the vicinity of Queen Anne's Creek is lacking. By the spring of 1737 the Chowan Grand Jury found the jail at Edenton to be "insufficient", saying that anyone committed to the jail "is a[s] freed."[35] This insufficiency led in 1738 to an Act of Assembly which allowed up to £2000 current money to be raised from taxes (up to 2 shillings taxable per year for two years) to build a new jail and a brick office in which the records of the General Court could be safely kept. Necessary repairs to the Courthouse were also to be financed by this tax. Concerning the condition of the old jail, the Assembly echoed and amplified the Grand Jury's findings. The text of the Act describes a situation wherein people are encouraged to commit crimes due to the ease of escape from prison thus making the administration of justice ineffectual. [36]

Although the precise time of the construction of this new jail cannot be fixed exactly, events resulting from an action taken by the Assembly in 1741 not only limit the period of years in which the jail could have been built, but also help to disclose the locations of the various public buildings in Edenton. This Act of Assembly provides for the building and maintaining of a courthouse, prison, and stocks within every county. More importantly, it also requires that a parcel of land adjoining each prison, and not exceeding six acres be marked out and made available to all qualified prisoners not committed for felony or treason, primarily debtors, for their use during the term of their sentence. [37] A Chowan County Court order of July 1744 described the manner in which these prison bounds or rules were to be laid out. It also makes clear that the new Public Jail had been built by this time.

> Ordered that four acres at the corner be laid off in such a manner as to take in the dwelling houses facing the street on each side and that Mr. James Craven together with Abraham Blackall Esq/ be appointed to lay off the same likewise that ⅓ of the lots towards the front of the street on each side be taken in, including the houses as aforesaid and to run the line close on the backside of the new prison so far as the Council Chamber and Prison lots and to carry the same quantity of ground that is cut off from the back of said lots down to the water's edge fronting the courthouse lots and as much along the Bay St. as will make up said complement. [38]

No action was taken on this order until April 1747 when Andrew Richard petitioned the court for access to this area. [39] In response, the court reiterated its order for the bounds to be laid, and did so again in July, and again in October, by then increasing the area to the full six acres. Finally the plan was completed on 26 October 1747, and was reported to court the following January.

The courthouse is clearly shown on the southside of King St. at the head of what is now the Courthouse Green, occupying lot 5, or as it was sometimes (or soon to be) numbered, lots 5 and 6. This position is also confirmed by a Deed of Sale for lots 7 and 8 in the old plan from Roger Kenyon to James Potter, dated March 1728 and registered the following May, in which these lots are described as "adjoining the courthouse." [40] As for the location of the prison and Council Chamber, all that can be said with certainty is that they both stood on the North side of King St. apparently sharing the same lots currently occupied by the Old Chowan County Courthouse. Finding a line "close on the backside of the new prison" that marks off one third of the distance from King Street to the rear, or North edge of the lots seems to place the prison back off the street, to the rear of the Council Chamber, facing away from that building. The Chamber would then have faced directly across the street to the Courthouse. As we shall see, this positioning seems likely in view of later developments.

Returning once again to a consideration of the 1738 Act to Erect the Gaol and etc., the Assembly stipulated that the new jail was to be made of brick. Although Lawrence Landrckin's account for work done to the jail on 19 June 1746 included two bushels of lime for work on the gable, a day's wage for a laborer, and 15 shillings for a bricklayer,[41] it is apparent that the jail, like the Council Chamber was a frame building with a brick chimney. The Act also provided for the building of a brick office in which the records of the General Court could be safely kept. These records included all court papers and all of the journals of the assemblies as well.[42] Despite what might have been a problem of space, in addition to one of security as posed by a wooden building, this brick office was apparently never built. One reason for this may be that if the new construction was at all delayed, Edenton's requirements for the storage of records would have already changed. Prior to 1739 the General Court met exclusively at Edenton. After that date the court met at various locations. It was not until 1746 when circuit courts were established and Edenton became the seat of one district that a General Court once again met regularly in town.[43] Similarly, the General Assembly ceased to meet only at Edenton after March 1737. For the next four years the Assembly shuttled between Edenton and New Bern. In November 1743 the Assembly met for the last time in Edenton. The need for a separate building in which to store records would have by this time significantly decreased. The move of government offices out of Edenton would also have opened up additional space in existing buildings. As to the repairs to the courthouse also mentioned by the Act of Assembly, no details of this work have survived. It should be noted that there is a gap in the Chowan County Court minutes from January 1738(39) until January 1740(41).[44] After that there are references to various fines being applied towards repair work on the courthouse in April 1747 and April 1748, but that is all until the 1750's.

Even if Edenton was beginning to lose its singular position within North Carolina politics, it continued during this period to grow economically. As the center of the counties of the Albemarle region, Edenton was both the source and target of political tensions involving itself and the newer and quickly growing areas of New Bern and Cape Fear to the south. Disputes which had come to center on the fairness of the Albemarle's numerically superior representation in the Assembly culminated with the November 1746 Assembly called in Wilmington. Not a single Albemarle representative was able to attend, but with only 14 of 54 members present, the Assembly proceeded to conduct its business. As a region, the Albemarle officially withdrew from the Assembly which then went on to legislate equal representation among all of the counties. New Bern was designated as the new capital of the colony, and for seven years no new elections of Assembly members were called. An Assembly recognized by the entire colony would not again sit until 1754. Bishop Gottlieb Spangenberg, while visiting Edenton in 1752,

BISHOP AUGUST GOTTLIEB SPANGENBERG. The Moravian Bishop came to Edenton in 1752 to acquire land for a settlement in the western part of the colony from Lord Granville's agent, Francis Corbin. (Courtesy Museum of Early Southern Decorative Arts, Winston-Salem, North Carolina)

made the following oft-quoted comment on the situation in northeastern Carolina:

> . . . meanwhile they declined to respect any Act passed by the Assembly. So in some respects anarchy reigns in these older counties. There are many cases of murder and theft and the like, but no one is punished. The men will not serve as jurors, so when court is held for the trial of criminal cases, no one is there. If a man is imprisoned, the jail is broken open—in short 'fist law' is about all that is left. But the county courts are held regularly and matters within their jurisdiction are attended as usual.[45]

Perhaps the Moravian Bishop's statement is a bit exaggerated (his remark concerning a scarcity of craftsmen in and around Edenton is not very accurate), but his presence in Edenton does raise the matter of Edenton's mid-eighteenth century prosperity. Spangenberg had come to discuss with Lord Granville's land agent, Francis Corbin, the acquisition of land for what would become the Wachovia settlement in the western part of the colony. Granville had established the office in Edenton in the 1740's, and it drew commerce, money, and business to town. These were good times for Edenton. The Port of Roanoke, Edenton's harbor maintained a busy pace throughout.[46] During the mid 1750's several individuals who would come to be among Edenton's most prominent citizens arrived, including Samuel Johnston, Richard Brownrigg, and Joseph Hewes. Craftspeople of all kinds were doing business in Edenton and Chowan County, and many were doing very well.[47]

As the private sector grew, the public sphere, in terms of buildings and services also expanded and was improved. The new prison built by the mid 1740's has already been discussed. Court minutes show that on 21 July 1743 a tax of 8 pence per tithable was ordered for the purpose of building a "magazen" (magazine).[48] Again in October of that year Chowan's need of a public magazine and a store house in which to keep it is mentioned.[49] An account of Sheriff Peter Payne's with the county for a 5 shillings per tithable tax levied in 1743 for the purpose of "erecting a magazine" shows that £281..10..0 was collected, virtually all of which was spent on gun powder, bullets, and swan shot.[50] The location of the store house and magazine remains undetermined. Whether a separate building was constructed, or existing warehouse space was used is unclear. Later records from the nineteenth century do show that a Gun House did stand on the county land in front of the courthouse.

During the mid 1740's Edenton's system of warehouses for the storage and reception of goods included the upper, or Bennet's creek warehouse and what is referred to as the warehouse in Edenton, the Public Warehouse, or possibly the lower warehouse. Although the original location of this Edenton warehouse is unclear, we do know that in October 1749, William Bonner agreed to move it onto the courthouse lots closer to the ships and wharves. It took Bonner at least two and one half years to comply with the court order, but it appears that the building was moved by the summer of 1753.[51]

As Edenton grew commercially, the need for more warehouse space and wharfage also grew. In April 1756 the court acted to correct this deficiency. Contained within the following order is some of the earliest description of public building in Edenton.

> The court taking into consideration the necessity of a Public Warehouse and Prize House and wharf at Edenton Do order that a warehouse for the reception of tobacco be built on the court house lots of the dimensions of 60' x 45' be erected with a shed of 12' wide on each side of the same the whole length of the warehouse with three substantial doors on each side and they at each end the house to be 12 ft (Pitch?) with good locks . . . and to be made of a good frame . . . and to be covered with inch plank well shingled and a prize house of 15' x 12' to be covered with sufficient plank and shingles with 3 prizes at each end. And that a sufficient wharf 12 ft wide will be made opposite to this warehouse to run into the channel.[52]

A tax of 1 shilling per taxable for three years was ordered to meet the expense. Francis Corbin, Joseph Blount, Edward Vail, John Benbury, Dempsey Sumner, Joseph Hewes, John Halsey, James Luten, William Hoskins, or any five of them were appointed commissioners. Corbin would act as Treasurer for the project. A contract for the work was to be offered to the lowest bidder and would stipulate that all work be done by the 20th of November.[53] No record of who took this work has been found, but Gilbert Leigh was allowed a small sum of money by the court in April 1757 for "fixing a prize and Prize Post and fixing _____ scales."[54] Court minutes from January 1759(60) do confirm that these new warehouses were built. Also, they supplemented rather than replaced existing buildings. In October 1758 the "Old Public Warehouse" was described as being "in a ruinous condition", and was ordered repaired by Solomon King, Inspector of Pork. King was also to build a small shed to protect the warehouse's scales and weights.[55]

Existing reports of repairs to public buildings after 1750 begin to become more frequent and are often more detailed than before. The jail, typically a building which received much abuse, required many repairs in order to remain secure. Accounts of this work often provide important information about the buildings and on occasion reveal the names of the craftsmen who performed the work. Humphrey Robinson was a blacksmith who often worked for the county, many times on the jail, at the warehouses, or on the gates in the fences which then surrounded town. In October 1751 he submitted an account of work done on the jail in the spring and summer of that year. Of the £28+ total (Va. currency), over £23 went towards iron work weighing 380¼ pounds for two doors. There were also charges for 15 pound plates for the doors, hinges, and a bar and bolt for the window. Moses Wellwood, a carpenter, submitted a bill at the same time as Robinson for woodwork done about the jail, in this case for making doors. John Benbury, the sheriff, was allowed for two spring pad locks, and for 100 feet of seasoned white oak plank which was used to make the floors.[56] A tax of 1 shilling per taxable in the county was raised to cover these expenses. By 1753 Sheriff Peter Payne protested against the insufficiency of the jail, a call which echoes with astounding frequency throughout the Chowan County Court minutes. It was often the first official act of a new sheriff. Two years after Payne, Charles Blount reiterated the protest. Sheriffs William Halsey in 1760 and Joseph Blount in 1763 would follow in order. The cycle of protest, orders to repair, tax, and repair repeat several times in some form through the mid 1760's. An account of Joseph Blount's for work done during the years 1764-67 show that John Rombough did work on the jail totalling £10..10..0. Iron work was done by James Sanders. There were also charges for 100 shingles for the gaol chimney. Finally, the dimensions of the white oak plank used for the jail floor were 15 inches broad, 13 feet long, and 6 inches thick.[57] Gilbert Leigh worked on the jail during these years, and like Humphrey Robinson before him (Robinson died in 1752), Leigh was one of several craftsmen to whom the county often turned when there was work to do. Rombough also began to establish himself in a similar position beginning in the mid 1760's.

The courthouse was almost 35 years old in 1750. General Court for the District of Edenton met there as did the County Court, or the Court of Pleas and Quarter Sessions. Beginning in 1734 the vestry of St. Paul's Parish held meetings there. These occurred as often as four or five times a year and continued until St. Paul's was ready to be occupied, around 1760. Larger church meetings, including an annual Easter Monday Assembly of all freemen in the parish at which the vestry men were elected were also held at the courthouse.[58]

County records do not provide many clues regarding the appearance or arrangement of the courthouse. The presence of windows is first mentioned in an account of Humphrey Robinson's which was presented to the Court in October 1751.[59] In July 1753 the court ordered "the 4 windows of the courthouse to be repaired and glassed."[60] This is an uncommon order in that the

DRAWING OF ST. PAUL'S CHURCH AS PRINTED IN *HARPERS*, 1857. (North Carolina Division of Archives and History, Raleigh, N.C.)

court was rarely if ever so specific regarding the number of windows to be repaired. Furthermore, when window repair work was written up and reported to the court, it was on every other occasion done in terms of the number of lights, or individual panes of glass. The 'glassing' charge was also determined per light. It seems likely that the court was referring to windows, not lights, and that there were only four of them at the courthouse. Although there are no references to any brickwork, a brick chimney at the courthouse would have been most likely, and, if not original, then perhaps added at a later date. It is probable that the building was heated in some manner during the winter terms of court. Also, a brick chimney, as opposed to a wooden one, would have been important for the better protection of court and county records once brought to the courthouse for storage.

By 1756 substantial repairs to the courthouse appear to have been necessary. In that year the General Assembly ordered a tax of 8 pence per Chowan taxable for two years for the purpose of repairing the Courthouse in Edenton. In doing so, it described the building as being "in a ruinous condition and great decay."[61] An accounting of the courthouse tax collected in 1757 shows 1417 taxables (with 130 insolvents) paying a total of £42..18..0. Unfortunately the account is not specific in describing expenditures.[62] By 1760 another £20 was set aside by the court for unspecified repairs. Joseph Hewes, Thomas Benbury, James Craven, and Thomas Bonner were to act as commissioners for this project.[63] Further repairs were ordered to the windows and "the planks at the courthouse door" in October 1761. Sheriff Halsey's account some 18 months later simply claims £5..2..8 for mending the courthouse.[64] John Green (later a partner of Gilbert Leigh) and James Palmer were ordered in April 1764 to repair the Bar of the Court, to put up benches, and to mend and put up a door with a proper lock, for which they received £5..7..4.[65] No other details are available.

The year 1766 is important in the consideration of early public buildings in Edenton. In that year, the General Assembly provided the legislative impetus for a new courthouse. By this time the old one must have been both outgrown and beyond repair. The Assembly's action regarding the courthouse will be examined in the following chapter, but this Act, passed at the Assembly's November session provided for the construction of a new jail as well as a new courthouse.[66] As we have noted, a new prison was built in Edenton in the early 1740's, yet two orders recorded in the Chowan County Court minutes of the October 1766 session of Court refer to both a new and an old jail.

. . . ordered that Joseph Blount, Esq. Sheriff of this county repair and put in good order the new goal of this county . . .

. . . ordered that Joseph Blount rent out to the highest bidder or bidders one of the public warehouses and the old goal for the term of one year . . . and that the other warehouse be laid open as a Market House by the sd. Joseph Blount.[67]

If Edenton had a new prison in October 1766, why did the Assembly vote to construct a new one in November? In fact, there was no new jail in 1766. Certainly there was none in response to any action of the Assembly until the late 1780's. As we shall see, the Assembly continued to press for a new jail in 1773 saying that the provisions of the 1766 act were insufficient. Perhaps the new Georgian Courthouse which was built in 1767 cost more than was anticipated. There were no taxes introduced in the county for a new jail. Also, there is no record of construction to indicate a new jail (although there was also none in the 1740's). What then of the 'old' and 'new' jails? The answer seems to lie in the relative nature of the terms themselves. References to an "old goal" (sic) begin to appear in the mid 1740's. In October 1745 a tax of 8 pence proclamation money on all county tithables was levied to pay, among other items, "for repairs formerly done on the old goal."[68] Three months later in January 1745(46), Sheriff Payne presented an account in the amount of £20..2..6 for "sundry repairs and necessarys found for the old goal."[69] This was to be paid out of any surplus tax money or out of the following year's tax. It seems likely that this 'old jail', still standing into the 1760's, is the first Chowan County jail built in the early 1720's. Having been replaced in the 1740's, and outliving its usefulness as a secure prison, even a forty year old former prison would serve well as a warehouse. Regarding the location of this building, it is likely that it either always stood on the original one acre lot set aside for the courthouse on the south side of King Street, or that it was moved, much as William Bonner had moved a warehouse to a location closer to the Bay, possibly from the north side of the street when it was replaced by the 'new' jail in the 1740's. In fact, the Sautier map of Edenton from 1769 does show a small structure on the public lots in Edenton behind, that is, to the south of the site of the former courthouse. This would have been both the logical and 'traditional' placement of the jail in relation to the first Chowan County Courthouse. Also, references to the "old goal" do occur in the records through 1769, though not afterwards.[70] It would seem that the old jail lasted forty or forty-five years and served two succeeding functions. The new jail, set behind or to the north of, first, the Council Chamber, and then the new Chowan County Courthouse was apparently always used as a prison. It, too, stood for just about forty five years.

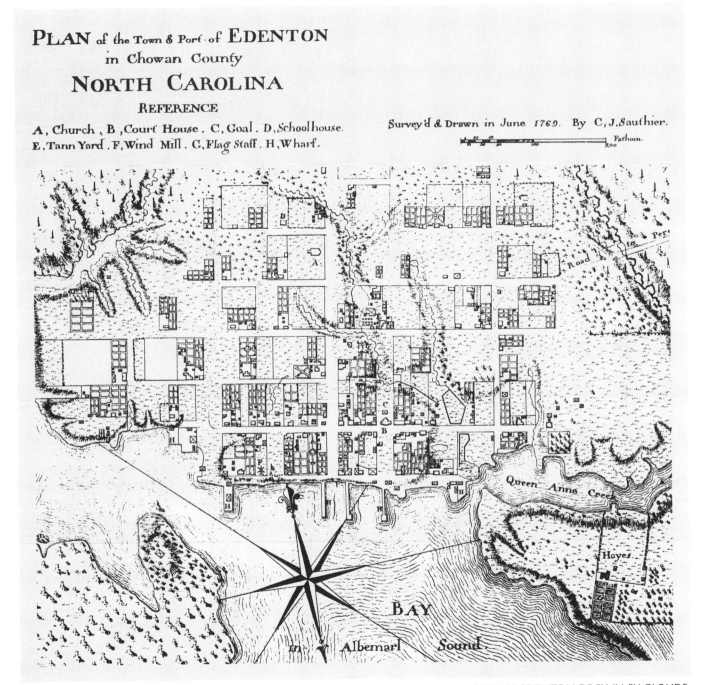

MAP OF EDENTON DRAWN BY CLAUDE
J. SAUTIER IN 1769

Edenton's New
Georgian Courthouse
1766-1806

The November 1766 session of the General Assembly passed a bill which had been introduced by Joseph Hewes and Jacob Blount providing for a new courthouse and new prison for the use of the District of Edenton. Cullen Pollock, Joseph Hewes, Thomas Nash, Edward Vail, and William Lowther were appointed commissioners to direct the project. The money needed to finance this construction was to come from several sources. A tax of 1 shilling per Chowan taxable, and 4 pence per taxable in the other counties of the District (Currituck, Bertie, Pasquotank, Perquimans, Tyrrell, and Hertford) was ordered "for the present and succeeding years." The Assembly also diverted to the construction of these buildings money which had already been collected by order of an earlier action passed in 1758 for the purpose of improving navigation in and out of Edenton's Port Roanoke.[1] This money, raised as duty on incoming vessels, was never spent as had been originally intended. Proceeds from the sale of "the old Court House, Prison, and other Public Buildings . . . standing on the Public lots in . . . Edenton" would help pay for the new buildings, as would any private and voluntary donations that could be collected by the Commissioners. The Assembly also required the Commissioners to report their transactions and accounts as the construction proceeded.[2]

Only three documents specifically pertaining to the building of the new courthouse have been found. The first is the Bond of the Commissioners with Governor Tryon in the amount of £2000. The conditions of the bond are, in effect, the successful completion of the provisions of the 1766 Act. Pollock, Hewes, Nash, and Vail signed the document which was left undated.[3] The second is a list of subscribers who contributed to the planned building. Twenty men pledged a total of £235, with William Halsey also offering one month's work of a bricklayer. The list is dated 25 May 1767.[4] Finally, the following notice appeared in the *Virginia Gazette* on 4 June 1767.

> To be let to the lowest undertaker on Thursday the 25th instant [June] at Edenton, in North Carolina, the building a brick Court-House 68 ft. by 45. The builder will be furnished with bricks and lime, and may depend on punctual payments. The trustees will attend with a plan of the house, and receive the proposals of such as incline to undertake the same. Bond with security will be required.

Cullen Pollock
Joseph Hewes
Thomas Nash
Edward Vail
William Lowther

At this point, perhaps it would be sufficient to remark on the curiosity that no further documentation regarding the actual building of the courthouse or the original financing of it has come to light. Of the architect or designer, builders or workers, there is no positive direct evidence. There are no drawings of the building (which the commissioners must have had by May 1767), no accounts with local craftsmen for original work on the building itself. Financial accounts of the kind required by the Assembly, or any other useful kind have not surfaced, either in the Accounts of the Treasurer and Comptroller's Office of North Carolina, the County Settlements with the State, Governor Tryon's correspondence with the Board of Trade in London or its representative Lord Shelburne, the records of the Colonial Office, or in any other British Records that have been examined. No account has been found in any of the Chowan County Papers, nor has there been so much as an off-hand remark made in any contemporary personal correspondence or paper yet examined on the questions, "Who designed or built the courthouse?", or, "How much did it cost?" The Committee of the Assembly charged with examining, stating, and settling the Public Accounts (of which Joseph Hewes was a member) presented a report on 5 December 1767 which lists only one expense for the Northern District under Public Buildings, the first £2000 allocated for Tryon's Palace, a structure designed and built by John Hawks, begun in the same year as the Chowan County Courthouse.[5] One factor which may have contributed to this lack of documentation may be reflected in Governor Tryon's own well noted dissatisfaction with the manner in which Public Accounts were being kept. Fraud among officials and a vagueness in the keeping of the public funds were among Tryon's concerns in 1767 and 1768.[6] But even this could not explain the lack of direct detailed information regarding the construction of the Chowan Courthouse. As for the minutes of the Chowan County Court, there is not so much as a mention of a new court house. In April 1767 Thomas Jones, Clerk of the County Court, was ordered to "rent a proper place for the reception of the records of this county."[7] As an indication that the buildings which were housing the records, the old courthouse and the Council Chamber, were no longer of use (actually about to be destroyed), this order does at least confirm that the county was looking ahead towards the construction of the new courthouse.

Although there are no detailed descriptions of the courthouse from this period, reports of repair work on the building do provide much useful information. Shutters on the windows were almost certainly present from the earliest days. They are first mentioned in a June 1775 court order to have them painted.[8] Three years later, in September 1778 the court directed James Blount, the clerk of the county court to have an unspecified number of new ones made and hung.[9] Another order from the June 1775 court term charged

LIST OF SUBSCRIBERS TO THE
CONSTRUCTION OF THE COURT-
HOUSE, 25 MAY 1767. (Southern Histori-
cal Collection, Library of the University of
North Carolina at Chapel Hill)

the sheriff to employ someone to tar the roof.[10] This was a common practice of long standing in an area where tar was in plentiful supply. Used on roofs along the east coast as early as the 1690's[11], tar was reported by William Logan on his 1745 visit to North Carolina to be in general use for weatherproofing houses.[12] In particular, it was used to help preserve and protect shingle roofs of the kind that originally must have covered the courthouse. Although documentary evidence showing the kind of shingle specifically used on the courthouse is lacking, it is probable that they would have been heart of cypress. Pine shingles were also commonly used.

Continuing with the outward characteristics of the courthouse, the upper stage arches of the cupola were originally glazed. The earliest reference to the presence of these windows occurs in 1785 when on 3 June thirteen lights were replaced.[13] Thomas Parramore reports that the cupola was illuminated on special occasions such as the celebration marking the adoption of the United States Constitution in December 1789.[14]

The cupola itself is the source of several questions. For example, when was the construction of the courthouse completed? The question of who designed the courthouse may also be raised here because of a drawing that John Hawks made in November 1769. The drawing is of a cupola that was originally intended for St. Paul's Church at Edenton, but which was never built there. It does, however, strongly resemble the cupola at the courthouse. The shape of the dome roof, a bit simpler in the drawing, is the only major difference between the two. The drawing shows a circular opening where the clock faces are now, but the original date of the placement of the clock in the cupola has not been firmly fixed. The shortness of the spire in the drawing, and its relative size to the ball which it supports actually describes what these features might have looked like before they were altered early in the 19th century. Was the courthouse still unfinished in the winter of 1769? Possibly. If so, was it being used. Apparently so. The cupola would have been the last part of the building to be built, and its construction would not necessarily have interfered with the court's conducting of business below. If Hawks' drawing did serve as a model for the courthouse cupola, why was it just being drawn in 1769, and why was it drawn for St. Paul's? On the other hand, if his drawing is a plan for a 'typical' cupola, is it possible that Hawks was suggesting that the church, as the other important and primary public building in Edenton have a cupola which in most ways matched its counterpart, perhaps already constructed (by Hawks?) at the courthouse? Unfortunately, at this point we can only note the resemblance and the connections between the two, and then move on.

The glass originally used in the courthouse may have come from England, but a more probable source was Philadelphia. With no specific document referring to the courthouse, the records of the construction at St. Paul's provide a contemporary example. But while John Benett wrote in February 1766 of the glass for St. Paul's that he was expecting to arrive from England, the Minutes of the church vestry report in May 1767 that a Mr. Swift was sending to Philadelphia for glass.[15] A study conducted by Colonial Williamsburg points out that window glass was only made by a few American manu-

CUPOLA OF THE CHOWAN COUNTY COURTHOUSE

JOHN HAWKS' DRAWING OF A CUPOLA FOR AN "EDENTON CHURCH", 22 NOVEMBER 1769. (Southern Historical Collection, Library of the University of North Carolina at Chapel Hill)

THE CHIEF MAGISTRATE'S CHAIR AS
VIEWED DOWN THE CENTRAL AISLE
OF THE COURTROOM

CHIEF MAGISTRATE'S CHAIR

facturers prior to the Revolution, but that by 1760 three firms were operating either in the Philadelphia area or in nearby New Jersey and Pennsylvania.[16]

The bricks of the courthouse were almost certainly locally made. The original floor of the courthouse is made of stone and extends the length of the courtroom.[17] It currently lies underneath the raised wooden floor in the room. In all probability, the stone came from outside of the immediate area.

The interior walls of the courthouse, with the exception of the Assembly Hall on the second floor, were probably plastered. Although there is no documentary evidence for plastering at the courthouse until the 19th century, it was a most common practice. As early as June 1774 the walls were whitewashed. A court order to that effect also instructs the sheriff to prevent people from playing games within the courthouse and from "daubing the walls thereof."[18]

The precise original arrangement of the courtroom is difficult to determine, but several details are either evident or may be reconstructed from the building as it appears today. The Chief Magistrate's chair in the rear apse of the building at the center of the raised platform which defines the Bar of the Court is more than nine feet tall. It must have commanded the entire room in the late eighteenth century to an even greater extent than it does now. The chair is surrounded by panelled wainscoting which once served as a backrest for the assistant judges of the court. These men sat on either side of the Chief Justice on a curved bench, traces of which are visible in the panelling. Supports for the bench are still in place on each side of the Magistrate's chair. The central stair leading up to the Judge's area is not an original feature of the courtroom. Following a traditional plan dominant throughout eighteenth century British courts both in England and the colonies, access to the platform was provided by two side stairs at either end. Also, the front of the platform itself did not originally run straight across the courtroom as it does now, but rather described a semi-circle parallel to the rear wall of the apse. This semi-circular wall is made of brick and is still in place underneath the present Judge's area. The front of the wall is still plastered, as expected, in keeping with the rest of the interior of the room.

The only reference to the arrangement of the courtroom from the documents of the time is a June 1768 court order which instructs Gilbert Leigh to make benches "near the Courthouse table for the Convenience of the Attorneys and Grand and Petit Jurors."[19] This suggests an area shared by the attorneys and the jury in the vicinity of a single table. This would be the area on the courtroom floor between the elevated bench and the area reserved for public seating or standing. The jury itself may always have been placed in rows to the side of and perpendicular to the Judge's area, roughly as it is today. Another possibility suggested by British and colonial practice would place the jury on a curved bench just inside the forward wall of the raised Judge's platform. The jury members would then have their backs to the judges, and would be facing the "courthouse table", the attorneys, and the public. However, given the small diameter of that forward semi-circle and the limited space involved, this seems a more unlikely possibility in the case of the Chowan County Courthouse. Another standard element of the courtroom, though not mentioned in the court records until 1809 is the clerk's table, possibly located on the other side of the courthouse table from the jury. If in fact there was originally only one central table, perhaps this table would have been shared by the attorneys and the clerk. There also may have been a separate place for the sheriff. Known as the sheriff's box, this feature was found in many eighteenth century courthouses, but no reference to a sheriff's box has been found among Chowan County records.[20] As has been indicated, benches rather than chairs were originally used for seating the court officials, with the exception of the Chief Magistrate. The public, separated from the place of official business of the court by a bar or balustrade, may have sat on benches placed on the stone floor, or may have been left to stand. In 1784, another table was ordered for use at the courthouse, and was to be made under the direction of Justices Michael Payne, Joseph Blount, and Stephen Cabarrus.[21]

The presence of a Franklin stove is first noted in June 1783 when the "Conductor of the Franklin belonging to the courthouse" was ordered to be repaired.[22] In June 1791, Joseph Blount, Clerk of Court, was instructed to procure a large Franklin stove from Philadelphia for use at the courthouse.[23] An account dated 9 February 1793 shows that John Hamilton bought a stove for the building from James Hathaway.[24] Hamilton lived in Edenton and operated several stores and warehouses around the coast of North Carolina.[25] He was also Chowan County Solicitor in the 1790's and early 1800's. The stove is described as "383 wt", and came with a length of (double?) pipe and its own mounting. It cost £15..0..1 in N.Y. currency, which after the exchange equalled £20..12..7 in 'paper'.

DETAIL OF THE MAGISTRATE'S CHAIR AND THE SURROUNDING PANELLED WAINSCOTTING. Traces of the curved associate judges' bench, removed in the mid nineteenth century, are still visible in the panelling, as the bench legs are still in place on either side of the chair

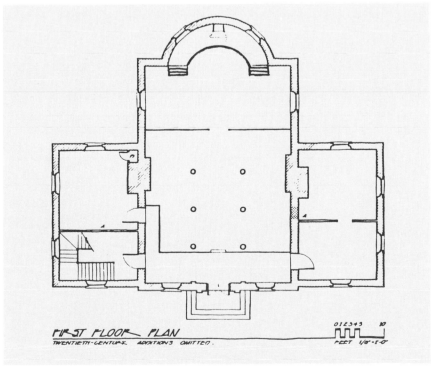

FIRST FLOOR PLAN
TWENTIETH-CENTURY ADDITIONS OMITTED.

ALTERED DRAWING OF THE FIRST FLOOR OF THE COURTHOUSE. The curved line in the area of the Bar approximates the original semi-circular configuration of that area. (Original drawing measured by Carl Lounsbury, Susan Lounsbury, and Douglas R. Taylor, drawn by Douglas R. Taylor reprinted, by permission from Lounsbury, *Order of the Court*.)

AREA BENEATH THE JUDGES' BAR
BETWEEN THE REAR APSE WALL OF
THE COURTHOUSE AND THE BACK OF
THE INTERIOR SEMI-CIRCULAR WALL
WHICH ONCE DEFINED THE BAR

Information regarding the appearance and furnishings of the offices in the courthouse are also scarce. From an account dated 20 September 1770 Gilbert Leigh and John Green[26] were allowed £15..15..1 for work performed on the clerk's office. Since this September date only indicates when the account was presented to the court, there is no way of telling when this work was done. Because of the large amount of plank listed, possibly used for the floor of the office, or perhaps for a ceiling as well, it is possible that some of this material was used for original work to the clerk's office. The specifics of the account are as follows:[27]

Dr the County of Chowan in Acc't with Leigh/Green
1770

Sept. 20		
	To one bookpress for the Clks office	£ 8..00..0
	To one corner ditto for do	3..10..0
	To 476 feet of Inch plank 8/	1..18..1
	To 180 feet do Inch and Quarter plk 10/	18..0
	To 3 hinges 5/	15..0
	To 500 6d nails 8/	4..0
	To 200 Batts 5/	2..0
		15..15..1

In October 1770 Leigh presented another account showing expenses for a brass knob lock, 2 cupboards, 2 tablets, and the labor of installing the locks.[28] Again, a year later, Leigh worked in the Superior Court Clerk's Office pulling down and putting up a bookcase, for which he was paid £5.[29] In December 1794, to improve security at the clerk's office, a lock was put on the bookpress, and the window was fitted with a locking bolt.[30]

One peculiar incident involving the interior 'furnishings' at the courthouse occurred on the night of 22 November 1805. From the December term of court comes the following description:

> . . . that William Burke Boat Builder on the night of the 22 Nov. 1805 with force of arms _____ with Body of the County of Chowan did then and there wickedly and willfully break down and destroy the main door of the large room in the upper apartment on the Court House in Edenton in the county aforesd. being the House established by law as a public Court House. . . to the evil example of all others in the case offending and against the peace and integrity of the state.[31]

TRANSFER PRINTED CREAMWARE JUG. Made for William Blair of Edenton, most likely produced in Liverpool between the years 1795 and 1800, this jug displays a 'rough' depiction of the Courthouse at Edenton. Blair's brother George, a sea captain, may have provided the 'description' of the building while in England. (Courtesy Museum of Early Southern Decorative Arts, Winston-Salem, North Carolina)

Information regarding the original assignment of office space at the courthouse is incomplete, and to some degree may be inferred from later records. There are 18th century references to both the Superior Court Clerk's office and the clerk's office. The East office on the first floor was undivided at the time, and was probably used by both the Superior and County Court clerks. It is likely that both doors from this office into the courtroom (one presently exists, the other has been covered over) were original to the building. This arrangement does maintain a symmetry with the two doors on the opposite side of the room, one leading to the Register's office, the other to the stair hall. It can be inferred from later records that at some time before the 1840's one of the doors from the Clerk's office was simply not used, perhaps blocked off with furniture. The Register, as has been indicated, would have occupied the West office. The Sheriff and the Clerk and Master of Equity may have shared offices with these officials. Later records do place the sheriff in the East office with the clerks. The office of the Clerk and Master of Equity was located at various places in the courthouse and at the official's home. There is, however, no firm evidence that offices for either of these positions were located at the courthouse during this period. It should also be pointed out that in the 18th century it would not have been unusual for there to have been an overlapping between a designated office and a private home, even though the trend was towards a more thorough separation. But these governmental and judicial positions were part time jobs held by men who were primarily business men, planters and merchants. For example, in June 1783, the County Court Clerk, James Blount was ordered to keep regular hours in his office every Tuesday and Saturday.[32] Later, in December of that year, the hours were changed to Wednesday from 10 AM until 4 PM. Apparently in an effort to restrict court business to the courthouse as well as to provide for regular hours, Blount was also instructed not to remove any records from his office.

The second floor West office may have served several purposes. Small meetings could have been accommodated there. Almost certainly it provided space for juries once recessed. There is no evidence that any permanent county office was maintained there during this time.

The upstairs room to the East of the Assembly Room may have been used in a similar manner until 1778. In that year, the Masons of Unanimity Lodge #7 were given permission to occupy the room. The entry in the minutes of the Lodge for 6 July 1778 reads:

> An apprentice Lodge was opened in due form, when it being reported that the Justices gave leave the Lodge might be held in the courthouse. Resolved that the Lodge be moved, it was accordingly moved, when Br. George Russell presented the lodge with an elegant Master's Chair for which he received sincere thanks...[33]

The chair referred to in the entry is the rather extraordinary chair from the Masonic Lodge in Alexandria, Va. which had been used there by George Washington during an earlier part of the century. It had been brought further south for its protection during the war.

In fact, Edenton was a safe place during the Revolution. Although there were threats of British attack in 1779 after Portsmouth, Virginia was taken, and again in 1780 and 1781, these attacks never materialized. Despite Edenton's status as an important port, the only action seen in Edenton harbor occurred in 1781 when a lone British row galley made off with a schooner. The British crew was captured and put in the County Jail. The courthouse and the town as a whole passed unscathed through these years.

The general condition of the courthouse had deteriorated by 1778 to the point that the General Assembly acted to provide for repairs. The building was described in the Act passed that year as being "in want of some repairs which may now be done at a small expense but if neglected will require a considerable sum for that purpose."[34] The Act, which primarily called once again for a new Prison in Edenton, named Joseph Hewes, William Bennett, Charles Bonafield (Bondfield?), and Josiah Collins as Trustees and Directors for both purposes. They were to enter into Bond with the Justices of Chowan County, and would receive the tax which the Assembly ordered to be raised, or borrow sufficient funds in the meantime in order to complete the tasks. In March of 1779 the County Court directed John Green to put the courthouse "in proper and thorough repair."[35] At the same time it also appointed Green to care for and keep the courthouse for one year in what is the first recorded instance of an individual being hired for this job. His wage was to be no more than £10 per year. At the next term of court in June, the order was repeated. This time, in addition to naming John Green to see to the repairs, the court also referred to "the ruinous situation of the courthouse."[36] On 1 July the Commissioners Hewes, Bennett, Collins, Allen, and Lockheart signed a Bond in the sum of £5000 with the County.[37] Details regarding the work performed by Mr. Green, or proof that it was carried out have not been found. It is clear that taxes from the other counties in the district were collected for the Jail, and therefore the courthouse, under the provisions of the Assembly from the late 1770's to the mid 1780's.[38]

An Act of the General Assembly passed in 1782 regarding various matters in Edenton cited the "injured" condition of the courthouse and its lack of proper care. It charged the Commissioners of the Town to repair the building and to collect money for that purpose as necessary.[39] By September 1784 the County Court ordered a tax of 1 shilling per poll, 1 shilling per £100 value of

MASONIC CHAIR OF THE UNANIMITY LODGE #7. The chair once belonged to the Masonic Lodge in Alexandria, Va. where it had been used by George Washington. (Photograph courtesy of Colonial Williamsburg Foundation)

INTERIOR VIEW OF THE ROOF
FRAMING STRUCTURE OF THE
COURTHOUSE

town lots, and 4 pence per 100 acres in the county for the specific purpose of repairing the courthouse. Charles Johnson, Josiah Collins, and William Bennett were named as commissioners.[40] Joseph Hewes had died in December 1779. The following June, the Commissioners in charge of the funds designated for the Prison and the Courthouse were ordered to "make a return of the money" that they had received.[41] Between September and December 1785 an accounting of that money was drawn up and filed with the court.[42] In September 1787 the Commissioners for repairing the courthouse were ordered to produce their accounts.[43] Charles Johnson came to court in December and reported that he had never received any part of the tax which had been raised to repair the courthouse.[44] There is no further reference to the tax, Commissioners, or an overall attempt to repair the courthouse until 1806.

Except for Gilbert Leigh and John Green, the only other individual specifically named as having worked on the courthouse was Henry Cheshire, who repaired windows in the cupola in 1785.[45] Cheshire is named in the Court minutes as a house carpenter and house joiner.[46] He would also serve as jailer in the 1790's. Many craftsmen, including these three, are named as having done work for the county, often on the county jail. Many others are simply referred to as practitioners in the crafts and trades that would have been required for the building and maintaining of the courthouse. In the 1760's and 1770's John Rombough seems to have done more work for the county than any other single individual. When Rombough took L(ouis) Ming as an apprentice in December 1774, it was to teach the trades of joiner, cabinetmaker, and blockmaker.[47] His personal accounts with Joshua Bodley from 1769-75 show him mending tables, chairs, spinning wheels, and a gun; rehairing a fiddle bow, making a new bridge for a fiddle, making cases and boxes, and doing some leather work.[48] His work for the county included the building of a public ducking stool, stocks, and a pillory in 1767; and in 1770, another pillory, stocks, and a whipping post.[49] He often worked on the jail

INTERIOR VIEW OF THE ROOF
FRAMING STRUCTURE OF THE
COURTHOUSE

INTERIOR VIEW OF THE FRONT GABLE
OF THE COURTHOUSE

SAMUEL JOHNSTON. Nephew of the Royal Colonial Governor Gabriel Johnston, defacto governor in 1775, first U.S. Senator from North Carolina, Johnston presided over the meeting held at the Courthouse in 1783 to discuss the state's outlook on the plans for the new nation. (North Carolina Collection, University of North Carolina Library at Chapel Hill)

during this period, fixing the locks many times. The amount of money paid to Rombough during 1769-70 as shown on Sheriff Thomas Benbury's account is more than twice the next highest total, which belongs to Gilbert Leigh.[50] In 1776 he made the steps for the chair in the masonic lodge room.[51] John Rombough died in 1784.

Miscellaneous Papers from Chowan County show James Harrison working as a bricklayer in September 1764. Nathan Culler and Michael Welch also worked at that trade in 1767-68. Blacksmiths of the time include John Garrett, John Ellis, and John Weir.[52] All three of these men worked on the jail in the early 1770's. Weir apparently left Chowan County in 1777 for political reasons.[53] James Sanders, another blacksmith, acted as County Jailer for a time in 1768. Thomas Oldham was employed in 1778 to do metal and blacksmith work.[54]

Among woodworkers, Sam Black was a cabinet maker in the mid 1760's. Samuel Popping built a new set of stocks for the county in 1778.[55] In the early to mid 1770's several woodworkers helped to complete the interior of St. Paul's. Thomas Eccleston and Thomas Hunter were paid almost £27 and £40 respectively for their work. Thomas Williams laid tile, underpinned the staircase, and built the pillars at the church.[56] (A note on 'pillars': This term, which will also come up in connection with the courthouse in the next chapter is ambiguous. It may refer to a column, any free standing supporting post; or a fence post, particularly one made of brick. In the only explicit local reference that has been found, an article in the Edenton *Fisherman and Farmer* from 2 October 1891 speaks of "the pillars of the Episcopal Church fence.")[57]

The courthouse was used for other purposes besides those associated with the court and county government. As Higginbotham says in his introduction to *The Papers of James Iredell*, the courthouse was the "focal point of community social life."[58] Iredell mentions dances, receptions, and other entertainments occuring at the courthouse. *The State Gazette of North Carolina*, an Edenton newspaper, reported in February 1789 on what may have been an annual event when it told of a Ball held at the courthouse in celebration of George Washington's Birthday.[59] On 3 November 1788 the paper announced an evening at the courthouse exhibiting, "A Moral Serious, Comic, and Satiric Lecture on Heads." The show was to consist of "20 characters large as life, a variety of airs and songs, to which [was] added 13 portraits in transparent painting."[60] Not something anyone would want to miss! The courthouse was also the scene of town meetings and political discussions. Richard Dillard reports on a meeting of citizens at the courthouse in August 1774 at which the unjust imposition of British taxes were denounced, and the British Boston Port Act was condemned.[61] In 1775 the Chowan County Committee of Safety met to enforce the non-importation of British goods, a measure enacted by the First Continental Congress.[62] Another town meeting was held in 1783 with Samuel Johnston presiding, at which James Iredell offered several resolutions concerning the direction that the new nation should take.[63] Another Public meeting was held in January 1797 to discuss measures to "protect the public safety of the people of Edenton against conspiracy by unknown parties."[64] In all likelihood this refers to the threat felt by some members of the community regarding the actions and attitudes of the Quakers concerning slaves. The Quakers were accused of "inciting" slaves, often by setting them free.

Religious functions were also held at the courthouse, particularly when a traveling preacher of note came to town. Joseph Pilmore, a travelling Methodist minister came to Edenton on Sunday 20 December 1772. His journal records that he preached at the courthouse, and "found a great many people assembled, who all behaved with the utmost decency."[65] Aside from decrying the condition of St. Paul's, he made no other comment on the town. The Reverend Jesse Lee stopped in Edenton in December 1782 to assist in forming a new Methodist circuit in the area, but chose to preach at the church instead of the courthouse.[66] Francis Asbury made his first visit to Edenton on 24 December 1783 when he preached to a "gay inattentive people."[67] He returned to town on 10 March 1804, and made the following entry in his journal:

> After 19 or 20 years, I preached in the courthouse and many attended . . .
> I now know why I come to Edenton; that I might feel for the people and
> make an appointment of a preacher for them; but we must get a house of
> worship here of our own.[68]

On his way to a Methodist Conference in Norfolk, Asbury stopped again on 7 February 1806 to preach at the courthouse.[69] Thomas Coke paid a visit to Edenton on 25 March 1785. He was also concerned with taking the town up into the Methodist circuit. Coke had few complimentary comments for Edenton, its people, or its church, which is perhaps to say that he found it all to be fertile ground for his ministry. He did, however, say that "the people in general prefer the courthouse, which is an elegant place, so I went there accordingly and preached to a large congregation."[70] Edenton is first mentioned as a regular stop on the Methodist circuit in 1793. Enoch Jones officially formed Edenton's first Methodist Society in 1808.

Several visitors also passed through Edenton during these years and left descriptions of what they encountered. Ebenezer Hazard, a new Postal Route Inspector, visited in June 1777. He described the courthouse as "a decent two story Brick Building."[71] He noted the other buildings in town as being "in general low, wooden . . . and much scattered."[72] He was impressed by the rope walk which, by his report, was then being built to the east of Edenton by Joseph Hewes and his partners. Robert Hunter, son of a Scottish merchant arrived in town on 9 June 1786 and wrote the following description:

> The people are almost all merchants here. They reckon about 1000 to
> 1500 inhabitants in Edenton . . . The houses are mostly very indifferent
> and all built of wood . . . They have a tolerably good brick statehouse, a
> brick church and a market place . . . They have a noble ropewalk here,
> built before the war. Their prison is very indifferent: They are going to
> build a new one.[73]

JOSEPH PILMORE. A travelling Methodist minister, Pilmore preached at the Courthouse on 20 December 1772. (North Carolina Division of Archives and History, Raleigh, North Carolina)

FRANCIS ASBURY. Asbury visited Edenton on three occasions to preach at the Courthouse; 24 December 1783, 10 March 1804, and again on 7 February 1806. Regarding his first visit, he described the congregation as a "gay inattentive people." (North Carolina Division of Archives and History, Raleigh, North Carolina)

County Jail and Other Structures, 1767-1806

In September 1769 Sheriff Thomas Benbury was ordered by the court to have the county jail moved further back from the courthouse.[74] This suggests that the new courthouse was built on the part of the lot formerly occupied by the Council Chamber, and that the jail, set behind the chamber had to be moved to better accommodate the larger newer building. Benbury's account with the county for that year shows that Thomas Eccleston was employed to do the job, and that he received £8..10..0 for his effort.[75]

The difficulty experienced by the county in trying to repair the courthouse and build a new prison during the late 1760's continued through the war years of the late 1770's and the early 1780's. In March 1781 the County Court appointed Josiah Collins and William Bennett as commissioners specifically to repair the county jail, which was then described as "in a ruinous state", and unable to hold prisoners.[76] They were to draw on the County Treasurer for up to £1000 and to receive all voluntary subscriptions. Sheriff Edmund Blount was ordered in September of that year to effect repairs.[77] The Assembly acted again in 1782 to provide for a new jail in Edenton.[78] The text of the Act mentions allegations that the sheriffs of several counties in the District had neglected or refused to pay much of the money for the jail that had been collected under provisions of earlier acts. The administration of justice was also said to have come nearly to a "stand". A new tax was ordered. Officials were required to pay all money that had been collected on earlier occasions for this purpose. Commissioners Michael Payne, Joseph Blount, Nathaniel Allen, Samuel Dickenson, and Nehmiah Bateman were bound to Governor Martin in the sum of 5000 milled Dollars on 10 June 1783.[79] Sheriff Blount was again ordered to repair the jail by the County Court. Finally, after materials had been purchased by the county, and after the General Assembly passed one more act in January 1787 to raise sufficient funds[80], action was taken to build a new jail.

Accounts of two of the commissioners involved in building the new jail have survived. Both were presented to the court in December 1790.[81] Nathaniel Allen's account shows that Charles Sheeter(?) was paid £2..8..0 in 1786 for drawing a plan of the jail. Curiously, no one by that name is listed in any census for Chowan County or the surrounding area in the years around 1790. Other expenditures were for timber, nails, spikes, hinges, locks, and several large quantities of iron. Stephen Cabarrus received £300. A payment was also made to Henry Cheshire who apparently did much of the actual work on the jail. Allen's account listed total expenses of almost £669.[82] Joseph Blount's account simply shows another payment to Cheshire, and a total of just under £50.[83] The jail was a wooden structure built on or near the same site as the building it replaced. It is also about this time that the County Court Minutes fix the location of the new whipping post and public stocks by ordering them to be erected at "the most convenient place between the courthouse and the Prison." They were to be made of cypress.[84]

The only recorded instance of an attempted escape from this jail occurred on 21 February 1789. The *State Gazette* reported that at about midnight the inmates set fire to the building, but that a negro man passing by gave the alarm and prevented the escape. Little damage was done to the jail.[85]

By September 1794 Sheriff William Roberts protested against the insufficiency of the jail.[86] A tax was ordered the following June. In December 1795 Jacob Blount, the Treasurer of Public Building was allowed £35..16..8 for repairs to the jail. His costs included 315 feet of square timber, 93 feet of feather edge plank, iron work, and 16 and one half days labor of Joseph Bunch.[87] The jail was again seriously out of repair by 1804.

The existence of two other public buildings may be noted here, even though they were the responsibility of the town and not the county. We have already seen that in the mid 1750's a warehouse was converted to serve as a market. In 1782 along with other rules enacted to improve and regulate Edenton, the General Assembly instructed the town commissioners to erect a public market.[88] As is by now clear, action by the Assembly can only be counted on to demonstrate a need, not necessarily a following action. Robert Hunter mentioned a market place in 1786, but the phrasing of his comment frustratingly leaves us in the dark regarding the material used in the building; "a brick statehouse, brick church, and a market place."[89] In 1789 Samuel Lattimore repaired the "Market House" in Edenton, and received £26..10..0 for his work.[90] An account of John Little, Town Treasurer, with the Commissioners of Edenton for 1796 also refers to the Market House. The following items were listed for 1 April 1796:

> To cash pd. Arthur Howe for 1200 bricks for Market House Pillars
> To Jos. Collins for 200 same for completing pillars
> To ditto for hauling bricks from the wharfs and Lime from the Satterfields
> To cash pd. Welcom for underpinning Market House / acc't
> To ditto pd. Jim T_____[?] for 2 days attending Welcom about ditto
> To ditto pd. Wm. Satterfield for Lime for Engine House and Market / acc't[91]

It would seem that the Market House was being improved at this time , not newly constructed. There is no other reference to it on this account. And again, the term 'pillars' is ambiguous, and may refer to a fence post or a support for a shed roof, for example. The man Welcom is in all probability Joe Welcom, a skilled black mason owned by Josiah Collins.[92]

The Engine House referred to on the account just mentioned does appear earlier on the same account. On 23 February 1796 John Spooner was paid £10 "on account/agreement" for building the Engine House. Again, Welcom was paid £1..16..0 for underpinning, and Josiah Collins received £17..2..2 on account for lumber, nails, and bricks; and for building and underpinning the House. Jacob Blount also received £1..5..6 for work done on it by his blacksmith.[93] Later records do place an Engine House near the courthouse, on the county ground.[94]

One other important item related to the public buildings in Edenton involves a drawing and plan for a new prison produced by John Hawks in June 1773. This follows directly upon one of the General Assembly's calls for such a jail to be built. Hawks is perhaps best known as the architect or builder of

JOSEPH HEWES. Signer of the Declaration of Independence, prominent Edenton citizen, one of the Commissioners for the building of the Chowan County Courthouse, Hewes was the recipient of the letter from John Hawks that is reproduced below. Portrait by Charles Wilson Peale. (North Carolina Collection, University of North Carolina Library at Chapel Hill)

the Governor's House built for Governor Tryon in New Bern. The connection between Hawks and Edenton is particularly interesting because John Hawks was a man with the training, sophistication, and the capability of erecting a building such as the Chowan County Courthouse. His association with the highest levels of North Carolina government is evident. His drawing of a cupola intended for St. Paul's Church in Edenton dating from November 1769 helps to further establish his familiarity with the town, much as a letter written to Joseph Hewes on 29 October 1773 demonstrates his association with one of its leading citizens. In that letter, Hawks discusses an unidentified architectural project with which Hewes and Samuel Johnston are involved.[95]

Hawks was the right man in the right place with the right connections at the right time to be considered a candidate, even a likely one, for builder of the Chowan County Courthouse. Unfortunately, not one shred of documentary evidence has yet been uncovered to support such a claim. As for Hawks' 1773 drawing and plan for the prison in Edenton, the connection between that document and the jail which still stands in town today will be explored in the following chapter.

JOHN HAWKS' LETTER TO JOSEPH HEWES, 29 DECEMBER 1773 IN WHICH HAWKS DISCUSSES AN UNIDENTIFIED ARCHITECTURAL PROJECT. (Southern Historical Collection, Library of the University of North Carolina at Chapel Hill)

TRYON PALACE. Front elevation of the
Governor's Residence in New Bern as
drawn by builder John Hawks. (North
Carolina Division of Archives and History,
Raleigh, N.C.)

William Nichols, Ebenezer Paine, and Two New Jails 1806-1835

The Courthouse, 1806-1835

The exterior of the courthouse received substantial attention in 1806. A tax (1 shilling per poll, 1 shilling 6 pence per £100 value town property, 4 pence per 100 acres land) was ordered in March of that year specifically for the purpose of repairing the building.[1] William Nichols, already in Edenton, and directing renovations and repairs at St. Paul's Church, began work on the cupola on 20 September 1806. His account shows that a scaffold was raised and remained up for 36 days. The cupola was painted, the roof was repaired, and a new ball was fixed on the spire atop the roof. Nichols was paid for five days of his own labor at £1 a day, while an unnamed Frenchman who worked with him was paid for six days at 12 shillings and 6 pence per day.[2] Another separate record shows that an unnamed black man was paid 2 shillings and 6 pence cash for climbing up and removing the old ball from the spire.[3]

Nichols' account occurs along with several others which mention paint or painting at the courthouse. From October to mid-December 1806 the Commissioners paid, on several accounts, for 333 weight English white lead and at least seven and one quarter gallons of linseed oil.[4] In almost every case an expense for oil was paired with one for putty. This putty may refer to a quantity of premixed lead and oil, perhaps to a tinting agent. On a separate account, a slave named Christopher, belonging to Matthew Sawyer received 75 cents or 7 shillings and 5 pence per day for seven and one half days "painting the courthouse."[5] Also, cut nails are among the materials specifically mentioned on these accounts, all of which appear on John Little's account with the Town Commissioners in 1808.[6] Later records suggest that the cornice of the building was painted on this occasion, as well as the cupola. In addition to the tax which was raised to pay for this work, fees paid for licenses which allowed slaves to work away from their owner's homes were directly applied to these expenses.[7]

Work on the exterior of the courthouse and on the grounds surrounding the building continued in June and July 1807. Nichols was again at work or directing work which included replacing windows and "putting sills round the courthouse." His accounts show that he was also involved with erecting a pump and its frame in front of the courthouse, presumably on the Green. Six days labor of a black carpenter is included on the account.[8] Welcome, the black man who worked on the market house, and his sons were paid £1 on 31 June for "building pillars round the courthouse" and for furnishing lime for the job.[9] Possibly a series of brick posts, perhaps for a low fence, were built around the courthouse.

The following order was issued by the County Court in June 1816, "Ordered that the commissioners of the town of Edenton have the courthouse repaired and painted, also the Gaol, and a whipping post and pair of stocks erected, that the county trustee pay the expense thereof . . ."[10]

From the records, it is unclear what work was done to the courthouse as a result of this order. The only itemized expense that appears is for $51.55 spent on window glass for the cupola (8 inch x 11 inch lights) and for the rest of the courthouse from July to October 1816.[11] There were several large expenditures recorded in the accounts of James Creecy, County Trustee, for December 1817 and September 1818 totalling almost $900.[12] Unfortunately, no details except the amount of money spent and the fact that the entire amount went towards repair of the courthouse have survived. As we shall see, it is likely that a sizable portion of the total was spent on the interior of the building.

The cupola once again needed to be repaired by 1825, and the court wished that it be put in good order throughout. No changes in plan were ordered except the relationship between the size of the ball and the spire was to be altered. The spire "was supposed to be too short and too small to support the ball."[13] The court apparently decided to lengthen the spire. The job was to be let to the lowest bidder, and was awarded to John Cox on 16 July 1825 for a bid of $45.[14] He was paid $70 the following September for the repairs and for painting the cupola.[15]

The first reference to a clock in Edenton occurs on a receipt dated 1826 from Edmund Hoskins to James Bingham. The clock cost $44, and was at least partially paid for by the town.[16] Hoskins, who served the county as sheriff from 1807 to 1815 and would go on to become County Court Clerk in 1827 and also Commissioner of Public Building was apparently authorized by the town to make this purchase. The next reference to the clock occurs when Hoskins hired N. Howcott to work on the clock for $1 in October 1828.[17] A reference specifically to a 'town clock' appears in 1845 when Edward Brown received $12 to keep it in good order for one year.[18] No records exist to document the clock's placement in the cupola. However, a newspaper article from May 1856 does refer to a "town clock lying idle in the upper storey of the courthouse."[19]

Windows continually needed to be replaced to keep the courthouse in good order. Several accounts show that glass was either bought in New York, or at least paid for originally in New York currency.[20] Glass often had to be cut to fit, as in 1806 when Thomas Hankins cut the glass, and a man named London installed it.[21] In 1810-11 William Manning, a well known Edenton cabinet maker, submitted a bill for cutting glass for the courthouse windows.[22] Nine months after Henry Wills, the Clerk of Court, was reimbursed in September 1825 for two boxes of window glass for the courthouse, the following severe order was issued by the court:

Ordered that each and every person who may hereafter be convicted of breaking the courthouse windows by playing ball against the building or otherwise pay a fine of $5 for each pane of glass so broken. That every slave committing the same offence be punished by whipping not exceeding 39 lashes . . .[23]

Shutters were replaced or rehung on several occasions during this period. An 1832 order to hang shutters when the county had available funds suggests that this was not a repair of the highest order, and that on occasion the courthouse went without some of its shutters.[24]

Small repairs to the chimneys, fireplaces, and the brickwork at the back of the courthouse were done by David Dickerson in 1835.[25]

It became apparent to the court in the early 1830's that measures to fireproof the courthouse should be taken. In June 1833, Joseph Manning, Commissioner of Public Building, was ordered to find out how much it would cost to cover the roof with zinc.[26] By the following May, Manning had died, and the court ordered Edmund Hoskins to have the courthouse covered with either zinc or tin, whichever was most cheap and durable. He was also authorized to borrow money against future taxes in order to complete the job.[27] Sheriff William D. Rascoe was brought in to assist Hoskins in November 1835. The two of them were ordered to proceed with as little delay as possible. The fiasco which ensued will be taken up in detail in the beginning of the next chapter.

Other repair work was also performed on the courthouse. Accounts with James R. Creecy, County Trustee from 1815 to 1824, show that John Littlejohn received $296.75 for repairs to the courthouse on 1 December 1817.[28] In September 1818 he received an additional total of $600, also for courthouse repairs.[29] There are no other accounts or references in the court minutes that could explain these large expenditures. There is only the order

VIEWS OF THE COURTROOM FROM THE BAR LOOKING TOWARDS THE REAR OF THE ROOM

of June 1816 to generally repair the courthouse. There are, however, the series of columns in the courtroom that were apparently not original to the courthouse. These six columns, perhaps built to add support to the ceiling, represent an expensive project. Stylistic details in the capitals of these columns suggest the work of William Nichols. An Edenton resident from 1806 until about 1818, Nichols built several houses in town, took on apprentices, bought and sold property (including slaves), administered wills, filed a petition to become a naturalized citizen of the United States, and as we have seen, did work for the county. He was also paid in 1811 for building a Baptist Meeting House in either Edenton or the surrounding area.[30] James Johnston engaged Nichols in 1815 to build the plantation house at Hayes, a job which took most of the next two years. Certainly in William Nichols, a builder who in the early 1820's would re-model the North Carolina Statehouse in Raleigh and then design the state capitals in Alabama and Mississippi, Edenton had a builder very able to design and complete these columns. Furthermore, the only other likely time for the construction of these columns occurs in the 1840's when once again much work was performed on the interior of the courthouse. The records for these repairs are more complete than earlier records, and do not mention the columns even though they do state quite clearly that the courtroom ceiling was to be replaced. Still, regarding the columns and Nichols' possible part in their construction, no direct documentation has been found to allow an unequivocal statement fixing the exact date or other details of their construction.

In a related note, one possible partial explanation for the lack of documentary evidence for this work may lie with James Creecy himself. Although the court ordered periodic inspection of Creecy's accounts, we have seen that these accounts with the county tend to present dates and expenditures, but not specific items or purposes. Official reports to the court were beginning increasingly to take this form. The individual accounts which might then

CAPITAL OF ONE OF THE COLUMNS IN THE COURTROOM. Stylistic features suggest the work of William Nichols

have remained with Creecy may simply have died with him. Creecy's apparent suicide in Baltimore in 1829 as reported by the *Edenton Gazette*[31] may have contributed to a final disarray of his papers.

During this period, the position of keeper of the courthouse became a more regular positon annually appointed by the court. Often an official of the court, this person had general responsibility for keeping the building clean, and for tending to the windows and doors. Sometimes the 'keeper' simply made sure that this work was done, usually by someone else. On other occasions the person was hired to do these tasks him or her self. (Elizabeth Bond took over for her husband Henry in 1817 and 1818.) From the accounts of Hezikiah Gorham, who kept the courthouse from 1809 to 1814, we finally find direct evidence that the walls of the courthouse were plastered. Expenses reported in September 1812 show nine days work for cleaning, plastering, and whitewashing the walls, along with the purchase of a quantity of whitewash and lime.[32] A blacksmith's bill for window stays is included. Also appearing on the account is a curious charge of "2 barrels had for stage burnt by the jury".[33] If this is a reference to a raised platform for the jury in the courtroom, it is the first and only such reference until the 20th century. Evidence that the ceiling of the courtroom was plastered appears in a court order from December 1826. On that occasion, a leak in the roof of the rear apse damaged the ceiling over the "judges" seat. The plastering was ordered mended and whitewashed.[34]

Other information regarding the interior of the courthouse includes an account dated March 1809 from Jacob D Moad(?) for plank used in mending the clerk's table.[35] Edmund Hoskins paid Gus A. Johnson in April 1835 for two writing benches with plank tops, possibly to be used by attorneys in the courtroom. The cost was $6.[36] Another permanent item in the courthouse was the jury box, in this case a wooden box containing the names of citizens eligible to serve on juries. William Nichols replaced the lock and the lid on the box in 1807.[37] The lock was changed again in 1810. This would obviously be another small recurring expense for the county. The offices at the courthouse remained simply furnished with a desk, bookcases, and book or paper presses. William Manning made bookcases for Elisha Norfleet at the Clerk's office costing $20 in 1807 and $10 in 1809.[38] The Register's office received a desk and bookcase in 1810 for $12.50.[39] Manning also made a paper press in 1810 for the records and papers belonging to the Court of Equity at a cost of $22.50, or as reported to court, £11..5..0.[40]

A project of transcribing old records and books which had begun at the courthouse just before the turn of the century continued into this period. One person was paid to do the copying while another was paid to examine and compare the transcriptions with the originals. Payment was accorded by the document or page. It would seem that neither the recopying of records nor any number of bookpresses aided the Superior Court Clerk in keeping order in his office. In June 1829, the court noted that the office had been "in a deranged state for many years", and remarked upon "the difficulty that any record or papers filed . . . can be found."[41] James Wills, the Superior Court Clerk, and Malachi Houghton were instructed to put the office in order.

They were allowed $300 for their efforts in December 1830.[42]

The only apparent changes in the allocation of office space at the courthouse involved the Court of Equity. It is clear that the records of this Court were kept at the courthouse in 1810 when William Manning made a bookcase for them. But the years 1827 and 1828 were active ones for Thomas Blount, the Clerk and Master of Equity. The 26 January issue of the *Edenton Gazette* reported that Blount had "removed his office to his dwelling house, where those persons having business with him can always find him."[43] A March 1827 court order instructed him to move his office to the West room on the second floor of the Courthouse.[44] The June court of 1828 found this arrangement to be "incompatible with the due administration of justice" because it restricted or prevented the suitable accommodation of juries, and endangered the building because of an increased chance of fire (a more prominent use for the room would have resulted in a greater need to heat it, thus the risk of fire), and greater exposure to weather.[45] Blount was told to move. The court does not say where the office was to be relocated. In fact, there is no further mention of this office at the courthouse until the mid 1840's. Also during this period there is no record whatever of the sheriff having any kind of office at the courthouse. That, too, does not occur until the 1840's.

DRAWING OF HAYES PLANTATION AS PRINTED IN *HARPERS*, 1857. (North Carolina Division of Archives and History, Raleigh, N.C.)

SEAT OF JAMES C. JOHNSON, ESQ

The responsibility for renting the rooms of the courthouse for special events and occasions officially rested in 1824 with Henry Wills, County Court Clerk and keeper of the courthouse.[46] That duty was shifted to the Commissioners of the Town of Edenton the following year,[47] but Wills' appointment specifically mentions dancing schools and public exhibitions as among the parties who may wish to use the rooms at the courthouse.[48] The available rooms were the West office and the Assembly Hall on the second floor, and the courtroom itself. Among the events which seem to have taken place yearly were a July 4th celebration, which in 1808 consisted of a 2PM dinner at the courthouse, preceeded by a ceremonial firing of cannon[49]; and an evening ball in honor of George Washington's Birthday, which in 1809 was reportedly "attended by a numerous and brilliant assembly of ladies."[50] An exhibition by students of Edenton Academy following their annual examinations took place "as usual" at the courthouse on 1 September 1808, and consisted of "orations, dialogues, and dramatic pieces spoken by the students."[51] Dancing schools were a fairly consistent tenant at the courthouse. They are mentioned in 1810, when William Clay was the sponsor[52]; 1819, with a Mr. D_____g in charge[53]; and 1828, when one was run by P.H. Anderson.[54] Anderson's school also sponsored dances or "Cottillion Parties" at the courthouse. Certainly, the Assembly Room is a wonderful place to hold a dance. Other entertainments, such as plays, were also performed at the courthouse.

Religious events continued to be held at the courthouse. In August 1809 the local Methodists planned to hold a two day meeting there.[55] A Baptist minister, James Woodberry, addressed the Edenton community at the courthouse in 12 October 1810.

The major social event at the courthouse during these years was President Monroe's visit in April 1819. Unfortunately, the town newspaper which covered this event was restrained in its reporting. Monroe arrived in Edenton accompanied by his private secretary; the Secretary of War, John Calhoun; and Mrs. Calhoun. His primary purpose for making the visit was to investigate the possibility of re-opening Roanoke Inlet through the Outer Banks, thus providing a much more direct shipping route from the ocean to Edenton. The article in the newspaper mentioned a 21 gun salute fired upon Monroe's arrival and an invitation extended to him to attend a public dinner at the courthouse.[56] Details of this event were promised in the next issue of the paper, but did not appear.[57]

County Jail and Other Structures, 1806-1835

This was a busy 30 years for jails in Edenton. Sheriffs William Roberts and Edmund Hoskins protested against the insufficiency of the jail and their own liability for escapes in September 1807 and March 1808 respectively.[58] The General Assembly passsed an Act in December 1807 to provide for the repairing, or if necessary, the rebuilding of the jail in Edenton.[59] Josiah Collins, John Skinner, John Little, James Hathaway, and Baker Hoskins or any three of them were appointed commissioners to examine the jail, determine its condition, and decide what action to take. They were authorized to build a jailer's house in addition to a new jail, but it is unclear whether one was built at this time. A yearly tax of no more than 3 shillings per poll, 3 shillings per £100 value of town property, and 8 pence per 100 acres of land was also authorized by the Assembly. This was precisely the tax ordered by the County Court in June 1808.[60] Commissioners Collins, Little, and Hathaway reported to the same term of court that rebuilding the jail was not yet possible, and that more than one year of tax would be required to meet the expected expenses.[61] On 20 January 1809 the following notice appeared in the *Edenton Gazette*:

> The Altering and Repairing of the Jail of Chowan County will be publicly offered by the Commissioners at the Jail on the 11th of next month between the hours of 11 and 12 o'clock and given to the lowest bidder. The alteration and repairs to be made, terms of payment, &c may be known by applying to
>
> John Little—One of the Commissioners[62]

At some point after the notice appeared the commissioners decided to go ahead with plans to build a new jail rather than repair the old one. A contract was awarded to William Nichols, who received his first payment of £288..14..6 on 19 July 1809.[63] Perhaps it was with this job in mind that Nichols advertised in the Edenton newspaper on 25 August 1809 for "one or two Negro Boys to serve as apprentices and to learn the business of a carpenter."[64] Another payment of £301..17..9 was received on 12 June 1810.[65] The minutes of the County Court from September of that year show that four black men had been sent from Chowan to the Perquimans County Jail and then returned.[66] This may indicate that the jail was not yet built by the summer of 1810. But by the following summer prisoners were being held, and in fact repairs were being ordered.[67] Nichols received his final payment of £158..0..2 on 9 June 1812. This brought the total spent on the jail to £1050. The full jail tax as authorized by the Assembly had been levied for four years, and the commissioners' account showed a surplus of £113..2..0.[68]

Records show that the new jail was wooden, two stories tall, and had (at least, but probably only) four rooms. After June 1812, Nichols repaired a hole made in some part of the upper story left by prisoners who had escaped. An undated reference to these repairs appears on the commissioners' account, and may refer to an escape mentioned in the Court Minutes in September 1815.[69] Because the account is itself undated, (although it appears not to have been presented to the court until September 1818),[70] it is difficult to determine an exact sequence of events. The account also shows that Thomas Bissell repaired the "large locks" on the front door of the jail.[71] The same court order from September 1815 also instructs the sheriff to provide substantial window shutters for the lower story of the jail, and to have them padlocked every night when prisoners were being held.[72] Other materials used in repairs to the jail included a quantity of plank, some specifically 14 inches wide; and 10½ pound, 14 inch long iron plates, which along with an iron wedge may have been used on the doors.[73] In 1817, holes were put into 42 pounds of iron, possibly for some kind of grate.[74] The usual charges for spikes and nails appear. The court order from June 1816 that has already been discussed regarding the courthouse also charged the Commissioners of

FROM *THE ESTATE OF CAPT. EBENEZER PAINE*, 22 SEPTEMBER 1829. Entries for 22 December 1826 and 20 November 1827 show payments made for building the Chowan County Jail. (North Carolina Division of Archives and History, Raleigh, N.C.)

Edenton to paint the jail. Records from June 1819 show that four rooms at the jail were cleaned by an unnamed black man, and whitewashed by Old Welcome.[75] Others who worked on the jail during these years include a blacksmith named A.D. Sheele[76]; John Standin and a black man named Tom, probably both carpenters[77]; and Cornelius Leary. Leary, who had been released from an apprenticeship to William Nichols in 1812 performed work on the jail on several occasions.[78]

A covered drain leading from the jail was constructed in July 1819. This drain, possibly a replacement or improvement upon a ditch which had been cut and covered with 200 feet of plank in 1817[79] required 4400 bricks and 5 days work from Joe Welcom to complete.[80] Josiah Collins was paid $37.05 for the materials and Welcom's labor (valued at $1.25 per day).[81] Jailer Abraham Howitt received $54 for other necessary unspecified materials.[82]

The court issued an order in June 1819 to have a fence "half enclose" the jail. It was to be 15 feet high, use the best 10 inch square post oak, and be built with four 6 inch square rails, and one and one half inch cypress plank. Spikes were to join, fasten, and cap the fence.[83] Three years later, with the fence not yet built, the court slightly changed its specifications so that the fence would completely enclose the jail. It was to stand 15 ft. from the front of the building and 10 ft. from its rear. Heart of pine was allowed to be substituted for the cypress plank.[84] The job was to be offered immediately to the lowest bidder, and completed by December. It is not clear whether this fence was built before the jail burned down in the fall of 1824.

The first indications that the jail built by Nichols was no longer usable occur in the Court Minutes for the December term of court in 1824. On the 13th of that month, John B. Blount, Nathaniel Bond, Baker Hoskins, and Ebenezer Paine were appointed to report back to court a plan for a wooden jail with an attached jailer's house. A tax of 20 cents per $100 value of town land and property and 30 cents per Chowan County poll was ordered for the purpose of constructing the new jail. Prisoners were ordered to be taken to the jail at Plymouth. Jonathan Houghton, Baker Hoskins, Ebenezer Paine, Ephraim Elliot, and James Bozeman were appointed as Commissioners to award a contract for the construction of the new jail, and to direct its completion. Before the December term was over, the Commissioners were themselves directed to seek plans for both a jail of wood and iron and one of brick and iron. The contract was to be let on or before 10 January 1825. If an acceptable plan for a brick jail which cost within $1000 of a wooden one was submitted, it would be accepted.[85] The Court Minutes for March 1826 identify Ebenezer Paine as the contractor.[86] An earlier entry in the Minutes from September 1825 empowered the commissioners "to sell the iron that was saved from the ruins of the old jail which was burnt . . . ."[87]

Laid in English bond, Paine's brick and iron jail was apparently completed, or nearly so, by July 1825 when Nathaniel Bond was paid $279 for building a fence around it.[88] This is the jail which stands in Edenton today. Paine also built a jailer's house which has since been replaced. Ebenezer Paine died in September 1826 before he received full payment for his work. A "2nd installment of [the] contract for building a Jail in Chowan" in the amount of

CHOWAN COUNTY JAIL. Built by Ebenezer Paine in 1825, it stands directly behind the Jailer's House on the Courthouse lot.

$1456.56½ was paid to his estate on 22 December 1826. The balance on the contract, $912.21 was paid in November 1827.[89] A total expenditure of approximately three to four thousand dollars may also be indicated by a sum total of $3644.42 borrowed by Paine on three notes from the State Bank which are listed among the debits on his estate.[90]

Paine owned approximately 325 acres of land in Chowan County and a house on two lots in Edenton on Eden Alley. A blacksmith's shop stood on his land, and a set of blacksmith's tools were among those items sold after he died.[91] A prosperous man, he owned 33 slaves, and was at least 45 years old in 1810 according to the census taken that year.[92]

The resemblance between the jail built by Paine and the drawing of a jail for Edenton made by John Hawks in 1773 has been noted on several occasions. An article in a 1972 issue of *Southern Antiques and Interiors* called the resemblance "striking".[93] Even though the author of the article was mistaken in believing that the jail was the one built in 1787 or 1788, a question raised in the article concerning the possibility that Hawks' drawing may have been somehow used as a basis for the jail is still pertinent. Certainly there are similarities between both two story brick buildings, one drawn, the other built. Major differences also exist. However, in all likeilhood, Ebenezer Paine did possess Hawks' drawing when he built the jail. It, along with other papers related to John Hawks were given to the Southern Historical Collection at

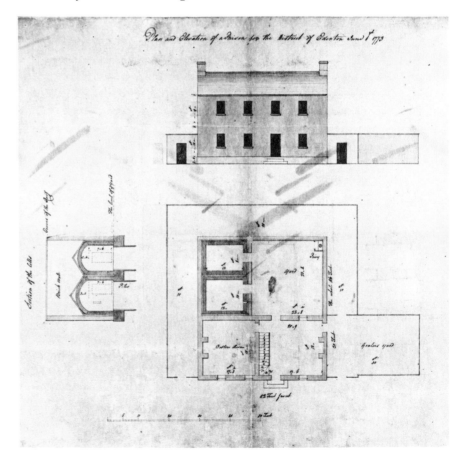

JOHN HAWKS' DRAWING OF A JAIL FOR EDENTON, 1 JUNE 1773. Hawks' description of this plan appears on the following page. (Southern Historical Collection, Library of the University of North Carolina at Chapel Hill)

John Hawks' References to Edenton Prison

After the foundation of the cells are laid and before the timbers of the floors are fixed, it may be a necessary precaution to drive poles close to the walls on the inside and 3 or 4 ft. below the foundation to prevent undermining in case the floor is broke up or any person on the outside should attempt giving assistance. The tops of these poles after drove should be level with the underside of the oak joist that re_____ the floor, and the joist about 10" square should bear at each end as far in the wall as the stone work is thick and not more than 6" assunder. the floor laid in the cells should be of 3" oak plank well spiked down with a plow(?) groove in each edge and an iron hoop put in lieu of a Tongue and 2 or 3 iron hoops on the top of every joist before the floor is laid to prevent working with a saw. The part shaded black in the middle of the _____ round the cells represent oak scantling about 6" sq. and should be framed and fixed when the timbers for the floors are laid and worked up between the stone and brick to receive the roof of the cells. Iron hoops should be be _____ to every angle of these pieces, the 11" brick wall then continues the height of the plan of the Roof of the front building. The part yellow is intended stone work from the top of the floor to the spring of the arches about 7 ft. 6 in. the arch to rise 3 ft. in the largest and 2 ft. 6 in. in the other [(of 2 cells)] as described in the section. The roof over the cells should be very secure and as near the top of the arch as possible and gutters wrought out of the _____ to convey the water thru the wall to the outside of the prison. The doors to be two thicknesses of in. and a half oak plank. The locks made for that _____ should be fixed in the doors and a strong iron plate over the lock on the inside _____ door _____ on and provided the door opens on the outside a cross bar with a strong pad lock make it yet more secure as one half the substance of the door case may be worked between the stone and brick of the walls it will be proper to fix the hooks before the door case is put up.

The debtors room will be _____ and lined with inch and a half or two inch oak plank and the joists of oak not more than 8 inches assunder and laid with iron tongues if thought necessary. The sashes are intended for 12 squares of glass only 8 x 10, the sash frames of solid oak worked in the wall, the sills 2 inches wider than the wall is thick and 6 inches thick on the inside and 3 inches on the outside. the head and jambs are (governd) by a sufficient substance to receive the iron bars and sashes To the 2 windows in the debtors room will be 7 upright one and a quarter inch irons bars set arris and let through flat bars 2 or 3 in number which flat bars are well secured at each end of the sides of the sash frame. In the other window in the jailers appartment 5 inch upright bars will be sufficient as they are more for appearance than real service. The sashes to be fitted in on the outside the upper sashes in the Debtors room drop down 8 or 9 inches, the lower sash fixed. the other sashes in the usual way. The court yard may be lined 10 ft. high with inch and a half oak plank to prevent the brick wall being broke through. The privy if not laid with very large stone should be (laid) with timber of the in or outside.

I have placed the chimney at the end of the debtors room to make the elevation appear more uniform, but as it is impossible without a considerable quantity of iron work to make it as secure as any other part of the room, have dotted it against the party wall (interior wall) where if thought most advisable it may be erected with out the least inconvenience save that of appearence which in a prison may not be so much considered. It may be necessary to erect a fence about 10 ft. high round the walls of the prison, likewise continue it a described for a yard a proper place for firewood or for the sleepers. The dimensions of the several rooms and height of the storys are figured in the drawing.

the University of North Carolina at Chapel Hill in 1857 by Robert T. Paine, Ebenezer's son. It is also quite likely that Ebenezer was related to Michael Payne, who in 1782 was one of the Commissioners charged with building a jail in Edenton, and in all probability did at one time have Hawks' 1773 drawing in hand. Michael Payne did have one son over 16 years old in 1790, and Ebenezer is listed with the last name 'Payne' in the 1810 census.[94] (Ebenezer's son Robert T. makes the point in a letter dated 28 March 1832 that his last name is 'Paine' not 'Payne'.)[95] Ebenezer's prosperity, and the very small number of Paynes or Paines in the northeastern part of North Carolina also suggest his connection with Michael Payne, himself a son of a former Chowan County Sheriff of the 1740's, Peter Payne. Michael Payne, a prominent Edenton individual who owned 27 slaves according to the census taken in 1784-87,[96] was also a Mason, a Justice on the Chowan County Court, and a U.S. Marshall for the District of North Carolina. Unfortunately, the vague circumstances surrounding Michael Payne's death have so far made a conclusive connection between the two impossible to determine.[97] Still, Hawks' drawing did probably provide a basis for Ebenezer Paine's jail of 1825. The descriptive plan which accompanies the drawing also gives us much useful detailed information about techniques employed in the construction of a late eighteenth century prison.

As for the new jail, few repairs or alterations seem to have been necessary during the remaining years of this period. The jail and the jailer's house joined to it were ordered to be painted in December 1826.[98] A new floor was laid in nine days in November 1834 by Tom, a slave owned by A. Moore; another man named George, and William Rea.[99] The November 1834 term of court also ordered a sufficient number of air holes, each the size of one brick, to be put in the walls of the jail under the [second] floor to increase air circulation.[100]

One incident in the early life of this building which is worth noting occurred in the late summer and early autumn of 1831. Fearful reaction to Nat Turner's slave revolt in nearby Southampton County Virginia is certainly apparent in the records of Chowan County. The *Raleigh Star* reported that "about 21 Negroes have been committed to jail in Edenton on a charge of having been concerned in concerting a project of rebellion."[101] In his history of Chowan County, Thomas Parramore quotes a similar number.[102] The County Court Minutes for September 1831 show that a new tax paid per slave was ordered with the proceeds going to fund Patrol Committees. New and stringent rules restricting the movements of slaves, to be enforced by these patrollers, were enacted by this session of court.[103] Tighter, more specific controls were ordered in March 1832.[104]

The most significant information regarding other public buildings in Edenton during these years concerns the Market House. A notice from the Commissioners of Edenton appeared in the 7 July 1808 issue of the *Edenton Gazette*, and announced that a contract for the building of a new Market House would be let to the lowest bidder on the 15th of the month.[105] A plan of the building had already been drawn, and was available to all applicants. This may have become the building shown at the lower end of Broad St. on the map of Edenton made by Augustus Gaylord in 1872[106] which currently hangs in the Register of Deeds office at the New Chowan County Courthouse. The position of the building is largely substantiated by a 1833 reference in a contract offered by the town for "filling up the lower part of the street opposite the Market House as far out into the bay as the embankment or wharf that has heretofore been made."[107] This building, as shown on the Sanborn Maps of Edenton from 1885 and 1893 was one story tall and measured approximately 55 feet x 20 feet. Late nineteenth century references indicate that the building was arranged with a series of stalls on either of its long sides from which merchants could do business.[108]

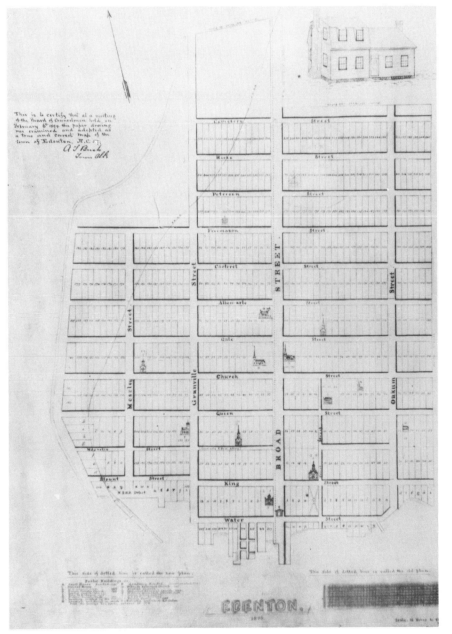

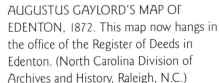

AUGUSTUS GAYLORD'S MAP OF EDENTON, 1872. This map now hangs in the office of the Register of Deeds in Edenton. (North Carolina Division of Archives and History, Raleigh, N.C.)

Roofs, Roofs,
and Renovations
1835-1868

The Courthouse, 1835-1868

Chowan County's decision to replace the courthouse roof began innocently enough with a court order in June 1833 which instructed Joseph Manning to "ascertain what it will cost to have the House covered with zinck and render the Court House fireproff (sic) . . . ."[1] The first indications that preparations for this work were being made occur in mid November 1835 when Edmund Hoskins, Commisioner of Public Buildings, bought pine and cypress plank from James C. Johnston for a stage to be set around the courthouse.[2] Laborers were paid for raising the stage and stripping the courthouse of its old roof.[3] In preparation for this project, taxes for Public Building had been raised from an 1832 level of 2 cents per poll and 1 cent per $100 value of land and town property to 20 cents per poll and 6 cents per $100 value in 1836.[4] The county offered the contract for the job to the firm of Houghton, Booth, Boardman, and Noble. Jonathan H. Houghton and Robert H. Booth were two Edenton merchants who had been in business together for some time. Boardman and Noble were from New York, and were relatively new partners in the company. An invoice from the company to the county shows that solder, solder mixture, zinc nails, and five barrels of zinc were put on a boat bound for Edenton from New York on 10 December 1835.[5] Elias Hatfield, the superintendent of the project arrived from New York with four workmen in early January. Fifty squares and seventy one extra feet of zinc were used on the job. Approximately forty days later Hatfield and his crew were finished, and returned to New York. Hoskins' account of the job shows a total cost of about $1650, most of which was payable to Houghton and Booth. This amount was covered by money raised from the 1834 Public Building tax and a loan to the county of $1077 from Joseph Coffield.[6] In October 1836, a balance of approximately $279 remained to be paid to Houghton and Booth. The Sheriff was ordered in February 1837 to pay that balance.[7]

By late summer in 1837 two things had gone wrong. First, Houghton and Booth had gone, or were going bankrupt to the detriment of many people in Edenton. Secondly, the new roof on the courthouse was found to be inadequate. At the very least, it leaked. Beginning in August 1837 the Court Minutes are full of cases filed against Houghton and Booth for debt. Both men were in jail for a time. In 1838 a judgment was made against Booth for not truthfully disclosing his assets.[8] Dr. James Norcom of Edenton described the overall situation in a letter to his daughter on 23 May 1837:

> . . . and that none of us has suffered materially from the derangement
> which had lately taken place in the business and trade of the county. The
> failing of the House of Houghton and Booth in this place had injured a
> great many people in the community, and ruined some; and, before break-
> ing they borrowed so much of the people's money that the article of cash
> has become quite scarce in the county.[9]

The August 1837 court ordered Sheriff Rascoe to find someone to repair
the roof, specifically to make it water tight.[10] Possibly because action against
Houghton and Booth was futile, the November court authorized Rascoe to
take action to "compel Elias Hatfield to account for damage to the County of
Chowan sustained in consequence of the careless and unworkmanlike
manner in which Hatfield performed his contract with the County in
covering the courthouse with zinc."[11] It is unclear whether any such action
was taken or was successful.

In response to the August court's order to repair the roof, Rascoe went to
Norfolk to find someone to re-cover the courthouse with zinc. Stages were
again set around the courthouse. The zinc was sent from Baltimore, and
William Delaney arrived with two men from Norfolk to do the job. Old zinc
stripped from the building was sold to John Cox for $2. H.W. Collins bought
the unusable lead for almost $7.[12] Delaney was finished by the end of
September. He presented a bill totalling $824.27 for labor and materials,
including 74 squares and 24 feet of zinc at $4 per square.[13] In November 1837
the court ordered a tax of 25 cents per poll and 10 cents per $100 value of land
and town property in addition to the Public Building tax (5 cents per poll, 2
cents per $100 value) already levied. It also authorized Rascoe to borrow
money against this collection in order to pay Delaney.[14] The entire amount
of his bill (along with $105 for other county expenses on the project and a
new whipping post), was borrowed from James Coffield.[15] Delaney's acount
was fully paid by November 15th.[16]

Two years later in November 1839, the court again had to order that the
roof be examined. It also authorized the Treasurer of Public Buildings to
contract for its repair.[17] The February 1840 court appointed Rascoe, John
Cox, and Jacob Parker as a committee to undertake this task, and to determine whether the roof should be repaired or replaced.[18] A local carpenter,
Rigdon M. Green was employed to assist in the examination. The committee
presented its findings at the next session of court:

> We . . . report that on examination of the frame of the roof . . . we found
> it considerably decayed, so much so that we think it necessary that it
> should be stripped entirely of its present covering to the frame, in order to
> more fully ascertain its condition for repairs. From information and experi-
> ence it is ascertained that a tight roof cannot be made with zinc, and we
> therefore recommend that it be covered either with shingles or slate.
> There will be considerable repairs of woodwork necessary to the other

parts of the building and most of the plastering to be made anew—and from best opinion we can form at present do suppose that the cost will probably amount to $2500.

3 May 1840 John Cox Wm. D. Rascoe[19]

The court went on to order that a new roof of cypress heart shingles be put on the courthouse, and that all work recommended by the committee be performed. Public Building taxes ordered by the court for 1840 totalled 30 cents per poll and 10 cents per $100 value of land and town lots.

It is not exactly clear what happened to the roof next. Jacob Parker, one of the members of the committee did receive what appears to be the first installment of the estimated $2500 needed to repair the courthouse.[20] Extensive repairs to other areas in the courthouse are recorded. It would seem unlikely that these repairs to the interior of the building would take place before the roof was fixed. It is also clear that the Grand Jury reported to the August 1847 court that the building was "in a leaky condition", and that the court ordered the clerk to inform the sheriff to repair the problem.[21] In August 1848, a committee of Thomas Warren, John Cox, and Samuel Bond was appointed to examine the roof and report to the next term of court.[22] At about the same time, the Grand Jury issued their report accusing the Magistrates of neglect of duty for not having the courthouse repaired.[23] At the November Session, Thomas Warren, Charles Nixon, and James Norcom were named as a new commission to offer a contract to have the roof repaired.[24] At some point between November 1848 and August 1849 a new shingle roof was put on the courthouse. Receipts from August 1849 show that $60 was paid to Spruill and Morse of Plymouth, N.C. for 15,000 shingles used to roof the courthouse.[25] A newspaper article from the 1940's reported that these shingles were uncovered when a later roof was being removed and replaced. They were described as being from 22 to 24 inches long.[26] The records do not indicate what, if anything, was done to the second zinc roof from 1840 until 1848-49.

As reported earlier, the clock in the cupola was kept in good repair in 1846. Some ten years later, on 8 May 1856, the *American Banner* described it as "now lying idle in the upper storey of the courthouse", and suggested that with a little trouble and expense it could again be put into operation.[28] The first reference to a bell specifically in the cupola occurs in the Court Minutes of March 1858[29], although a November 1831 order describing punishment for slaves found "by the Guard after the ringing of the bell"[30] may also refer to the bell at the courthouse. The concern in 1858 was whether the bell should be rung at the opening of County and Superior Court terms. The matter was to be taken up with the Town Commissioners. Another matter concerning the courthouse bell involved its removal from the building during the Civil War for use in making cannon. Several town and church bells were melted down for this purpose, the result of which was the formation of the Edenton Bell Battery. Richard Dillard reports that the courthouse bell, along with that from the Academy, Hotel, and other private bells were used to manufacture a gun named "The Edenton." Bells from St. Paul's, the Methodist Church, and from the shipyards owned by T.L. Skinner and R.T. Paine went towards the casting of the guns known as the "St. Paul", "Fannie Roulhac", and "Columbia" respectively. Dillard names the Richmond, Virginia foundry, the Tredegar Iron Works, where the cannon were made, the dimensions and commanders of the various guns, and the battles in which they served.[31] Curiously, in telling the same story, Thomas Parramore mentions only three cannon, leaving out the "Edenton", and making no mention of the courthouse bell.[32] The court records also fail to say anything about the removal of the courthouse bell, but here too, the matter may have been under the jurisdiction of the town, not the county. Town records for these years are not available.

Very little other work was done to the exterior of the courthouse during these years. There were the usual repairs to windows and shutters. Also, more information regarding which areas of the courthouse were painted becomes available at this time. Apparently, only the woodwork and not the brickwork was receiving paint. On 15 June 1836, M. Clark presented Edmund Hoskins with an account for a small quantity of black paint and putty bought for the courthouse from Will Badham for $1.65.[33] A second receipt dated five days later shows that M. Clark received $22 for painting the "cornis" and cupola of the courthouse.[34] This payment of $22 is also added on to the end of Edmund Hoskins' cumulative account with the county labelled "roofing the courthouse with zinc."[35] The cornice and cupola were painted at the same time. The black paint was presumably used on the cupola's roof, possibly the weather vane as well. We have already seen that in 1806, Christopher spent seven and one half days at 75 cents a day "painting the courthouse", also at a time when the cupola was being repaired.[36] William Nichols' account for the work done on that occasion mentions painting as part of his general description of the job.[37] Both Nichols' account and the payment for Christopher appear on Edenton Treasurer John Little's account with the Town Commissioners in 1808.[38] In May 1850, Isham Stewart was allowed $14 for eight days work "painting the courthouse."[39] It seems likely that both Christopher and Isham Stewart did similar, if not the same jobs, that is, they painted the cornice and cupola of the courthouse. In 1836, M. Clark may have overseen the operation much as Nichols did in 1806. An account from that year shows that Isham Stewart received $7.50 in March for six days unspecified work at the courthouse.[40] If this was a receipt for painting, as is likely, it would seem

M. CLARK'S RECEIPT FROM EDMUND HOSKINS FOR PAINTING THE "CORNIS AND CUPOLA" OF THE COURTHOUSE, 20 JUNE 1836 (North Carolina Division of Archives and History, Raleigh, N.C.)

to be the account for which Clark requested payment the following June.

Another major job which involved painting occurred at the courthouse in 1860. A contract for painting and refitting the building was awarded in August 1860 to G.W.F.D. Collins. His bid of $552 was to include $36 to John King, a black man, for making necessary repairs to the brickwork, and for whitewashing the interior of the building.[41] The job may also have included plastering inside, and possibly the painting of the Assembly Room.

The court's decision in February 1840 to investigate the advisability of abandoning the second zinc roof in favor of a shingle roof was part of a larger overall attempt to improve the courthouse. The Justices described the building as "in a dreadful state of delapidation and decay."[42] The May court ordered general repairs, and specifically instructed that the ceiling in the courtroom and the two adjoining offices be removed and replaced with one of plank.[43] This work, along with the work on the roof was to be funded by the $2500 which the Treasurer of Public Building was authorized to borrow. Also, the County Trustee was to pay all surplus funds, for example, that in the Jury fund, to the Treasurer of Public Building.

A committee formed in May 1841 was instructed to advertise and contract for the necessary repairs. A year later, R.M. Green was paid $300 as part of his contract. Unfortunately, no further details are given.[44] This is one particular example where the work performed may have been either on the interior or exterior of the building. Also at the May 1842 session, the sheriff was ordered to have the courthouse plastered.[45] In August 1844, Thomas Charlton, one of the Justices of the Court, proposed terms to have the courthouse lathed and plastered.[46] His proposal, to furnish materials and labor at cost ("a first rate plasterer for $1 per day, an apprentice at 25 cents per day) was accepted. In August 1845 Charlton was allowed approximately $180 for the repairs, which was to be paid when the county had the money.[47]

Were the ceilings on the first floor replaced with plank? The records do not directly say so. R.M. Green did do work on several occasions which is not described in any detail. A large quantity of plank was bought from John Thompson in December 1842, but this material may have been used in raising stages around the jail which received a new roof that month. More plank, scantling, flooring, and laths totalling approximately 1150 feet appear on an account with James C. Johnston in 1844. But this account, like several others from this time may not be particularly reliable indicators of when these materials were used. The county was short of funds, and a year or more may have gone by before any cash changed hands. Also, much of this lumber may have gone to replace decayed portions of the courthouse roof frame. It may be that only a careful examination of the ceiling itself will reveal whether the plaster ceilings were ever replaced with plank.

Another project was begun in February 1843 when the sheriff was instructed to conduct his business in the Superior Court Clerk's office. Accompanying this order was another to build a partition which would divide the office into two separate offices. The partition had no door in it. Also, the contractor was to have "both doors [of the original office] open into the courtroom."[48] This suggests that by 1843 there were two doors leading from the clerk's office

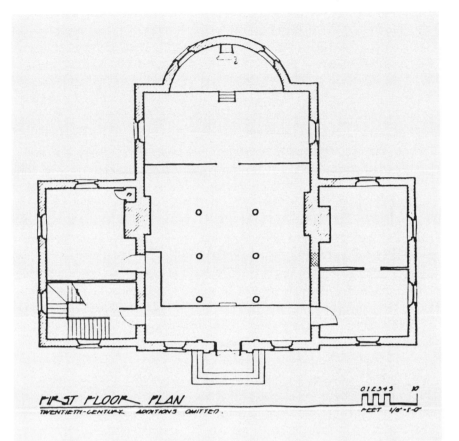

FIRST FLOOR PLAN
TWENTIETH-CENTURY ADDITIONS OMITTED.

01 2 3 4 5   10

FEET 1/8"=1'-0"

PLAN OF THE FIRST FLOOR OF THE
COURTHOUSE WITH TWENTIETH
CENTURY ADDITIONS OMITTED
(Measured by Carl Lounsbury, Susan
Lounsbury, and Douglas R. Taylor, drawn
by Douglas R. Taylor, reprinted, by
permission from Lounsbury, "Order of
the Court".)

and that both were original to the building. The second door, which has
since been blocked off, has left an outline which is visible in the courtroom
wall today. The two doors to the clerk's office are matched by the two openings on the west side of the courtroom, the entrance to the Register's office
and that leading to the stair hall. The order that would have "both doors
open into the courtroom" may suggest that one of them had not been in
regular use for some time. Although the court said that the sherriff's stay in
the clerk's office was to be temporary, records from 1846 and 1856 place his
office in the courthouse, sharing the east wing with the clerks.[49] These are
the first three indications that the sheriff maintained an office at the building. It appears that from 1843 to 1856 the Superior Court Clerk and the
sheriff shared one part of the divided office while the county clerk kept his
office in the other part.

In addition to the sheriff, Superior Court Clerk, County Court Clerk, and
Register, the Clerk and Master of Equity was also identified in the Court
Minutes of November 1846 as "occupying rooms" at the courthouse.[50]
Thomas C. Manning, the new Clerk and Master of Equity, addressed the
court in May 1849, and described the haphazard condition of the papers and
records of his office. He told the justices that he had provided himself with a
desk and locks for better securing of these records, and reminded them that
the Assembly had just required all Clerks and Masters of Equity to hold their
offices at the county courthouses. Manning therefore asked that a room be

assigned to him.[51] Alexander Cheshire, the Chair of the Court, was appointed in November 1850 to prepare an office "in some part of the courthouse" for that purpose.[52] In August 1852, Manning was authorized to share the Superior Court Clerk's office.[53] Three and a half years later, in February 1856, a door in the partition between the clerks' offices was ordered to be cut.[54] With no mention of the Clerk and Master of Equity, the Superior Court Clerk and the County Court Clerk were ordered to switch places so that the latter would share an office with the sheriff.

There were no major changes within the courthouse offices themselves during these years. Desks, bookcases, and presses continued to be the usual furnishings. Reference to candles, specifically to sperm(aceti) candles, appear on accounts dated February 1838 and 1839.[55] A stove was provided for the area occupied by the sheriff and the Superior Court Clerk after the partition of the clerk's office in 1843. Window blinds are identified as having hung in the clerk's office after 1838. Twenty yards of B____ Lace was bought for them in June of that year.[56] In August 1853, the court ordered an iron safety chest to be purchased to provide a safer means of storing records in the clerk's office.[57] A fireproof safe was ordered for use at the same office in May 1855.[58]

There were a few interesting incidents involving the records at the courthouse during these years. When William R. Skinner began his long tenure as Clerk of Court in May 1849, he reported that the Minute Docket had not been written up for two years, and that generally many of the records of the office were in an unsatisfactory condition. Skinner explained his own difficulty in clearing up the matter as being due to the state of affairs left by his predecessor. Specifically, Skinner was unable to get the slips of paper which had to be transcribed because many of them had been kept in the former and deceased clerk's hat until the time of his death.[59] Similarly, at the same session of court, T.C. Manning reported that upon taking office as Clerk and Master of Equity he received no records of the Minute Docket further back than 1816 and no records at all of the Trial Docket. He did say that he found a case of papers in "one of the rooms of the courthouse" that belonged to his office, but that since it had no lock on it, he could not be sure whether anything had been taken from it.[60]

After the beginning of the War Between the States, the Clerk and Register were authorized to remove the records from the courthouse to a place of greater safety.[61] Actually, the war years passed relatively quietly in Edenton which, along with much of Coastal Northeastern North Carolina came to be regarded as 'behind Union lines' very early in the war. Union gunboats first steamed into Edenton harbor in February 1862, and periodically returned, but by early 1863 all hostile units had left the county. No major engagements were fought in Chowan during the war. In August 1865, the court records were ordered returned to the courthouse.[62]

By the mid nineteenth century a marked change can be seen taking place between what had been a rather vague notion of the separation of private and public spheres, and a more definite and strict one. When it came to the attention of the court in 1846 that Superior Court Clerk Samuel T. Bond was using his office at the courthouse "for purposes of a private character and in no way connected with the business of the sd. office", he was ordered to discontinue his activities and remove from the office any "implements belonging to a private individual."[63] The court considered Bond's actions as threatening to the security of the courthouse, and specifically ordered all courthouse officials to confine their activities in the courthouse to the administration of their official duties.

The courtroom itself changed during these years. The first alteration, involving the placement of the stove gives a clue, although an inadequate one regarding the position of the jury within the room. In February 1842, the court ordered the sheriff to "have the stove removed to the center of the jury box and that he buy pipes for that purpose so that the pipes shall go across the house and in both chimneys."[64] John Morris received payment in October for stove pipe, and for cutting a hole in the chimney.[65] As for the location of the stove on the courtroom floor, the term 'jury box' may refer generally to the area between the Bar and the public seating. As an enclosed area in which the jury sat, it could. Or it could refer to a more particular portion of that area reserved for the jury alone. The description of the placement of the stove might infer a location roughly equidistant between both chimneys. Unfortunately, due to the lack of other references, speculation only results in more unanswered questions.

The Bar underwent a major change in February 1850 when chairs were substituted for the benches which had accomodated the justices of the court until this time. R.R. Heath and Augustus Moore were put in charge of altering "the present arrangement of the bar" which included this substitution.[66] Chairs were also brought in for the other officials of the court which had previously been seated on benches. More chairs were ordered for the court in November 1850, twelve of which were to be set aside for the jury.[67] Chairs bought specifically for the jury in 1853 are simply described on an account between the county and Shreiff T.S. Hoskins as "round back chairs" which cost $2.50 apiece.[68] The court is not specific about what other changes were made, but it must have been at this time that the raised judge's platform was extended and squared off, and that the two side stairs on either side of what had been a curved Bar were removed in favor of one central stairway. This central stair which perfectly frames the Chief Magistrate's chair may have been constructed to emphasize to a greater degree the status and power of that position, while the substitution of chairs for the single bench may indicate an increasing autonomy among the associate justices. The records do show that John G. Hankins, County Coroner, was allowed $24.50 in August of that year for work done in the courtroom.[69] A separate place for the Clerk is still indicated in a reference to "the seat of the clerk of court" in the Minutes from February 1852.[70]

Non-judicial activities at the courthouse of the kind already described continued during these years. In addition to holiday celebrations, local political nominating meetings were reported to have been held at the courthouse.[71] The Chowan Agricultural Society used the Assembly Hall for its regular meetings as of May 1855.[72] Coincident with the action taken to restrict private use of the building by public officials was an order issued in

February 1856 which required all private parties (except the Masons) who wished to use the rooms at the courthouse to first receive permission to do so from at least three County Magistrates.[73]

One of the most important public meetings held at the courthouse was convened on 12 February 1861. The subject of discussion was North Carolina's relation with the Union. John H. Leary presided over the meeting. The 'Unionist' majority position which advised "prudence and discretion", (as described by participant J.H. Garrett), was delivered by John A. Benbury.[74] The seccessionist candidate, John C. Badham, presented the minority opinion which favored immediate withdrawl from the Union. Garrett reports that a second minority opinion was offered by himself "deploring the sad national affairs", and urging adherence to the Union unless some overt act of provocation were to occur. The meeting was to select two candidates who would then be presented to the voters. The winner would be the representative to the State Convention. After John C. Badham was selected as the Seccessionist candidate, his supporters withdrew from the meeting. William E. Bond was then chosen as the Unionist candidate. At an election held in the county on 22 February, Bond won by a vote of 427 to 79.[75] Lincoln's inauguration and the attack at Ft. Sumter within the next few weeks left the results of the vote meaningless.

Although there was a Town Hall in Edenton, the courthouse was also used by the town on occasion. Town records show that a public meeting was held there upon the "cessation of the Provisional Government of the town of Edenton" on 30 January 1866.[76] A resolution was passed providing for the election of town officers.

As for judicial events, one of the most notable and notorious court cases in Chowan history, the case involving the will of James C. Johnston of Hayes Plantation, came to trial in February 1867. Brought to court by members of Johnston's family who had been left out of the will, the trial resulted with the will being upheld. Hayes was left to Edward Wood.

Finally, it should be stressed that aside from the events and meetings which regularly occurred within the courthouse itself, the building's role as the focus of community activity was never demonstrated to a greater extent than on those days which marked the opening of a new term of court. An anonymous visitor to Edenton in 1861 left the following description of the activity which accompanied one such day:

> People who have no court business assemble for the purpose of paying and collecting debts, purchasing mules, harness, and etc, making trades, talking politics, and too many, I fear, to have a spree. There is generally a smart sprinkling of drovers, horse jockeys, auctioneers of books and jewlery, gamblers, dentists, 'drummers' and daguerreotypists.[77]

In an unattributed comment, Thomas Parramore also quotes the following description of the hustle-bustle around the courthouse during court week in the middle of the nineteenth century:

Then you would find practically the entire adult male population of Chowan thronging the streets. Temporary booths for the sale of cakes, pies, and other refreshments, mostly kept by Negro women, abound in the neighborhood of the Courthouse and there are also numerous 'tobacco wagons' which resemble by their large size and huge canvas tops the Western Emigrant wains of earlier generations. The wagons were driven by nomadic peddlars from Granville Co. whose travelling shops dispensed the weed in quantities and qualities to suit any taste.[78]

County Jail and Other Structures, 1835-1868

Records from the late 1830's indicate that the lower floor of the jail was divided into "apartments."[79] A Grand Jury report from 1860 also refers to the "upper cells", indicating a similar arrangement on the second floor.[80] In all probability there were two rooms on each floor. The East room on the lower floor received the most abuse, and was in the most constant need of repair. It may have been the most frequently used room, and perhaps was designed to be the most secure. A debtors apartment, long a fixture at the county jail was still present in 1851.[81] The interiors of at least some of these rooms were lined with plank, possibly all of them, possibly the entire building. There were many orders issued during these years to have the interior of the jail white-washed. The roof was shingled.

An August 1837 session of court ordered the lower apartments of the jail to be repaired and made secure.[82] The resulting account between Jailer William Rea and the county shows expenses for 337 feet of plank and twelve days work by Moses, a carpenter who belonged to Stephen Elliot. (Elliot would become County Clerk and Master of Equity in 1839.) Also included were other bills for carpenter work presented by James Sansbury, Thomas Charlton, and James Bozeman. A $5 charge for "Building a Chimney" and charges which show that at least some of the windows were fitted with glass as well as iron grates are also listed.[83] Sheriff Rascoe, then also Treasurer of Public Building, was directed by the court in November 1842 to have the jail and the jailer's house "newly shingled."[84] Completed by the end of December, the job required 11,000 cypress shingles, and was performed by William Kirby.[85] Other improvements ordered by the court included a large window on the back of the jail in each of the lower rooms, ordered in May 1846.[86] These were to be the same size as those in front, and fitted with grates in a similar manner. A stove was ordered put in the Debtor's room in November 1851.[87] Several orders for stoves and pipe for the jail appear in the Court Minutes between August 1852 and May 1856.[88] In 1859, a lightning rod already in place on the jail was repaired.[89]

The process of erecting a wall to enclose the back of the jail began with a May 1846 court order which called for a 15 feet wall, spiked at the top, to be built 20 feet out from the building. In December 1852, Sheriff T.S. Hoskins paid for 52 juniper posts designated for the jail which may have been used for this purpose.[90] An account dated 1854 shows that the wall, made of wood, was built by a carpenter named George by December of that year.[91]

A Grand Jury which met in August 1860 reported on several ways in which security at the jail could be improved.[92] The purpose of the report was to suggest measures which could be taken to help prevent escapes and conversations between prisoners and persons outside the building. The attachment of the jailer's house to the jail was identified as a problem. A recommendation was made to move the house. The Grand Jury also suggested that the "fence" on the back of the building should be made to enclose the entire jail. They also noted that the square holes cut through the floor of the upper cells near the gable windows could be used to pass weapons down to the lower cells either through those windows or from the jailer's house. Connecting these ventilation holes with tubes would, along with the other suggested measures, prevent this from occuring. Although no specific record has been found regarding the moving of the jailer's house, the 1885 Sanborn Map of Edenton does show the building detached from the jail.

Other changes not specifically involving the jail itself include what may have been the building of a separate kitchen to serve the jail in 1838. In the first reference to such a structure, Sheriff Rascoe was allowed $42.94 for brick and timber in May 1838.[93]

There is not a lot of information regarding the other structures with which we've been concerned. Stocks and a whipping post continued to be fixtures in the town during these years. What appears to have been the last whipping post constructed in Edenton was put up in February 1854.[94] The court ordered the Town Commissioners in February 1861 to remove the Gun and Engine House "now near the courthouse off from the county ground at and near the courthouse."[95] They were probably moved to one of the Town Commons and remained under Town control. The Market house underwent repairs and alterations in 1866. The town council ordered that it be enclosed on the East and West sides (the long sides) "by a diamond latice work, the South end by the same including a folding door." The north end was to be repaired and fitted with a good lock.[96]

Status Quo:
Late 19th Century Edenton

By the mid nineteenth century, Edenton's economy and status as a town of importance in North Carolina had already undergone severe changes. Long before the disruptions of the Civil War in the 1860's had effected the state and the rest of the south, the basis of Edenton's eighteenth century commercial prominence had been devastated. The completion and established success of the Dismal Swamp Canal in the early 1830's made the long shipping route through the Outer Banks unnecessary, and had transferred much of the region's seabound trade to Norfolk, Virginia, the northern terminus of the system. Edenton and Chowan County were forced to find their economic sustenence in other areas. Recovery and change were slowed if for no other reason than because of growing geographic isolation. The failure of Houghton and Booth in 1837 had also been a serious blow to the local business community. Although the fishing industry, for example, grew tremendously during the mid nineteenth century, one finds many contemporary examples of a longing for the "old days". Writing in 1871, J.H. Garrett reminisced in lyrical fashion over the change in the town: "The thistle now thrives and the cattle leisurely graze without hindrance or let upon the wharves which were once covered with immense cargoes of produce, lumber, and merchandise."[1] A column printed in the Edenton newspaper *American Banner* on 2 October 1856, begins in a similar manner and then continues with a particularly stinging description of mid-century Edenton:

> Then Edenton harbor was filled with vessels coming to load and unload, and not as now, merely to lay in safety .. Then our wharves had a show of business activity and were covered with lumber and shingles, staves, and the produce of the Indies. Now they are rotting in the sun. Such Edenton once was and such she now is. Telling the inhabitants of their faults and exhorting them to arouse has no effect. They are bound up in the listless indolence of their present condition and we say let them alone. We have wrote our last homily to them. Enterprise and energy is a stranger that will never visit the place and if he does, he will stay only long enough to say 'finished town', and turn on its heels. The only jewel that adorned Edenton's crown has gone to another world and now avaricious indolence reigns supreme.[2]

Even J.H. Mullen, once mayor of Edenton, recalled his arrival in town in

1892 by saying: "None of the streets were paved. Its business was at its lowest ebb in history. It was said that no hammer had been heard in 40 years and it was perfectly apparent that no paint had been used in that period of time."[3]

Whether the caricature of Edenton that can be drawn from these statements is attributable to the condition or convenience of memory, the idea of a 'golden age', the grind of a political axe, or any other source is a question beyond the range of this inquiry. Certainly there were many economic changes in and around Edenton dating from the loss of traffic at the harbor by the 1830's to the establishment of other industries particularly towards the end of the nineteenth century. Social and economic conditions obviously changed following the war as the slave system was dismantled and replaced by a system of tenant farming, an institution 'peculiar' in its own way. But as measured by the business of county government, especially with regard to its public buildings, the situation, either in terms of growth or loss, did not undergo drastic changes. The county was sometimes "not in funds" simply due to economic hard times. Money was borrowed to pay for necessary projects. Buildings were generally maintained, though perhaps on occasion only after reaching what in earlier times may have been called a "ruinous coundition." Substantial repairs were made as needed, although, as before, several years were sometimes required before action was completed. Even though the jail received appreciable attention, it was not remodelled or rebuilt as recommended by the County Building Committee in 1885. But the jail was still in use into the 1970's, and was not equipped with steel cells until 1905.

The year 1868 was the year in which North Carolina adopted a new State Constitution. Among the changes brought about by this document was the abolition of the Court of Pleas and Quarter Sessions and the Court of Equity. Responsibility for the judicial functions performed by these courts were consolidated under the newly constituted Superior Court. The administrative functions of the County Court, including care, maintenance, and overall responsibility for public buildings passed to a Board of County Commissioners. The Chowan County Board held the first of its monthly meetings at the courthouse on 13 August 1868.

The Courthouse, 1868-1896

No major repairs or expenditures involving the courthouse occurred until 1885, although indications of two problems do arise prior to this. In September 1880, 1000 shingles, 30 inches x 6 inches, were ordered to repair a section of the building's roof.[4] By December 1883, another 2000 described only as "not heart shingles" were purchased for the courthouse.[5] These limited actions, directed at specific leaks, were found to be insufficient by 1885, and led to a more complete job. Another problem had to do with the foundation on the east side of the building. In December 1881, Jailer J.Z. Pratt was instructed to furnish lumber and dirt to correct the problem.[6] His February bill for $4 indicates a fairly minor repair, but it must be remembered that $1 still bought 100 feet of lumber in Edenton at the time.[7] As we shall see, this

CHOWAN COUNTY COURTHOUSE,
CA. 1891-1904 (Reprinted courtesy of
People's Bank, Edenton, N.C.)

COURT HOUSE IN EDENTON.

Built 1712, And Was Once Used Both as a
Provincial and State Capitol Building.

DRAWING OF THE COURTHOUSE
FROM THE *EDENTON FISHERMAN AND
FARMER,* 31 OCTOBER 1890 (North
Carolina Collection, University of North
Carolina at Chapel Hill)

DRAWING OF THE COURTHOUSE
FROM THE *EDENTON FISHERMAN AND
FARMER,* 15 NOVEMBER 1895 (North
Carolina Collection, University of North
Carolina at Chapel Hill)

problem was also more thoroughly corrected in 1885.

The Board of Commissioners and the County Magistrates first met in September 1884 to discuss the necessary repairs to the jail, jailer's house and courthouse. A report was submitted which recommended that the courthouse needed to be painted inside and out; needed new venetian blinds and window lights; the plastering was to be repaired and whitewashed, leaks in the roof fixed, lightning rod and weather cock repaired, and the roof painted with fireproof paint.[8] A contract for this work was to be offered to the lowest bidder. The Board was authorized to borrow sufficient funds. A total of over $1800 was borrowed from B.F. Elliot, R.L. Bunch, J.T. Stacey, and W.D. Pruden to help pay for the job.[9] At the next meeting of the Board, the commissioners decided to employ a "mechanic" to examine both buildings, determine which repairs were necessary, and to have the specifications drawn up. The report of the Building Committee which received the work on 4 June 1885 after it was completed by the contractor, Richard N. Hines, does not state these specifications. It does say that Hines was paid $1575 and was to have furnished all materials except paints, lime, oil, and cement. He was reimbursed $172 for these items. Other payments were received by Hines from 5 December 1884 to 1 June 1885.[10] It would seem that many of the repairs first suggested by the Commissioners and Magistrates were done. It is also clear that the courthouse was given a new tin roof. The Sanborn map of 1885 indicates that the courthouse had either a tin or a slate roof An article in the *Chowan Herald* of 25 July 1940 states that a tin roof was being removed from the building to make way for a new roof.[11] Pictures of the building prior to 1940 also clearly show a metal roof. No other roof was put on the building between 1885 and 1940.

Hines also did other work besides that originally called for in his contract. A brick wall was "built to the East of the courthouse to support the courthouse wall and prevent [its] undermining".[12] The charge was $50. A single course of bricks which may be remnants of this wall is visible in the ground to the east of the building. No record of the removal of this wall has been found, and it does not appear in any photograph of the building yet examined. The small coal shed which stands behind the courthouse was also built by Hines at this time. It also appears on the 1885 Sanborn map. The courthouse was fitted with gutters and rainpipe. In the courtroom, tables were made for the Bar. A chandelier was hung in the Assembly Hall. The Building Committee ended its report by congratulating Hines for a job well done, and by describing the courthouse as "now both a credit and an ornament to the county."[13]

The suggestion made by the Magistrates and Commissioners that the courthouse needed to be painted inside and out raises several questions. On those occasions when the courthouse was 'painted', what part(s) of the building received paint? Although the report of the work done by Hines in 1885 is not specific, drawings of the courthouse which appeared in the Edenton newspaper *Fisherman and Farmer* in 1890 and 1895 do show a building with dark trim contrasted against a light colored brickwork. This is the same scheme of light to dark that appears in the earliest photographs of the courthouse. These drawings are simple, but if the string course, arches, and water table were not, in fact, darker than the rest of the building, why would they be represented as such? It would seem that Richard Hines' work in 1885 probably included a complete painting of the exterior of the courthouse, and that the building was painted white or a light color. It could have been painted completely before this, perhaps as part of G.F.W.D. Collins' work in 1860, but here, too, specifics are lacking. As for the interior of the building in 1885, references to plastering and whitewashing do occur among the specifications of Hines' work, and afterwards. These later references specifically pertain to the offices and the courtroom where paint was apparently not introduced until 1911-1912. In all probability, the Assembly Hall was the only major interior portion of the building to have been painted in 1885.

The other major change at the courthouse involved the installation of a new clock in the cupola. Edenton's newspaper, the *Fisherman and Farmer,* began pushing for a new town clock in the mid 1880's. One column from 6 December 1887 suggested that if the county wasn't able to purchase one, then a private effort should be rallied.[14] On 5 June 1891, the paper reported that town council members W.I. Leary and A.H. Mitchell had been appointed to determine the cost of a clock, and to receive private donations towards its purchase.[15] By 4 September, they were authorized to purchase a clock and arrange for its placement in the cupola at a cost of no more than $550.[16] The county donated $20 in October to repair the cupola in anticipation of the clock's arrival.[17] The Council also authorized the purchase of a new bell for the tower, and ordered the town bell, apparently still in the cupola, to be removed and set uptown as a fire alarm.[18] On 30 October 1891, the paper reported that the clock had been put up during the previous week, and that it was working well.[19] This is the same Seth Thomas clock which sits in the cupola today, although it has since been electrified. M.D. Bradley of that company installed the mechanism. The bell, bought through Edenton hardware merchants Bond and Jones, is stamped with the date 1891, and was manufactured by the Shane Bell Foundry of Baltimore, Maryland. The newspaper reported that the bell weighed 523 pounds. The bell is currently

PLATE ON THE SETH THOMAS CLOCK IN THE COURTHOUSE CUPOLA. The clock was installed in Octoer 1891

THE COURTHOUSE BELL. Manufactured by the Shane Bell Foundry of Baltimore, Maryland, the five hundred twenty three pound bell was installed along with the Seth Thomas clock in October 1891.

struck from a fixed position, but the presence of a wheel and carriage, and a bell rope in the courthouse suggests that this bell (or its predecessor) was originally meant to swing as it tolled. Many of the counterweights from the clock may still be found on the top floor of the courthouse. The *Fisherman and Farmer* called the clock, "the biggest improvement in Edenton for years."[20]

All of the other work performed on the courthouse during these years was of a more minor nature. In the fall of 1869, Charles Blair and John Skinner were paid for materials, and John Hathaway, Phillip McDonald, John King, and Dorsey Stewart were paid for work. King, who had repaired the building's brickwork on previous occasions, worked six days. Stewart, who worked for five and a half days, may be related to Isham Stewart who painted "at the courthouse" in 1850 and, probably, in 1836 as well. He could also be the same person or be related to the Dorsey Stewart who would paint the courthouse in 1904. Phillip McDonald was paid for twelve days work. A total of about $75 was spent (not counting Hathaway's total which is illegible). The men were paid $2 a day.[21] Here again a painting project is suggested by the timing, the personnel involved, and the time spent on the job, but is not definitely indicated.

In addition to the work required by the installation of the clock, the cupola received attention on several occasions. W.F. Grubb was allowed $53 for putting a lighning rod on the courthouse, specifically on the cupola in January 1875.[22] It was repaired in May 1877, September 1885, and again during the summer of 1886.[23] In August 1887, Theo Ralph was ordered to repair the damage done to the cupola by lightning. He received approximately $42 for his work.[24] The lightning rod was removed from the courthouse in the summer of 1893.[25] A search through the newspapers from these years provides no details of what damage might have occurred as a result of the storm. It is possible that Ralph's work in 1887 included removing the windows in the cupola in favor of a permanent wooden or metal closure. Lights were still being replaced in the cupola in June 1881,[26] and as late as April 1886, Charles Leary was ordered to replace sashes in "the cupola windows."[27]

CHOWAN COUNTY COURTHOUSE CA.
1904-1910 (North Carolina Division of
Archives and History, Raleigh, N.C.)

CONTEMPORARY VIEW OF THE
INTERIOR OF THE CUPOLA LOOKING
UP FROM THE LOWEST STAGE
TOWARDS THE HIGHEST.
Note the old bell rope

CORNER SUPPORT IN THE LOWEST
STAGE OF THE CUPOLA

He was paid for changing three of those sashes the next month.[28] The Barden photograph of the courthouse taken prior to, but around 1910 does not show windows in the cupola. The cross pieces in the arched openings are far too widely spaced to be the muntins for individual 8 inches x 10 inches lights of glass. Not yet covered by the metal louvres which currently adorn the cupola, a more solid fixture is seemingly indicated. The old glass windows may, however, still be found inside the lower stage of the cupola. When further repairs to the cupola to correct its leaky state were found to be necessary by the Grand Jury in the spring of 1894, the matter was passed from the County Commissioners to the Town Council.[29] Upon examination of the interior of the cupola today, one immediately notices that its heavy vertical supports are frequently notched, seemingly to admit substantial horizontal braces which are no longer present. Exactly when and if these earliest supports were removed in favor of other means is unclear.

Maintenance of a more general kind included painting the new tin roof. This occurred in July 1886 and again in April 1893.[30] The color of the roof at this time remains undetermined, although a 'hand painted' post card from 1910 shows the courthouse with a red metal roof. (The card shows the courthouse painted white with grey water table, string course, and arches. The shutters are green).[31] As for the shutters, the commissioners ordered four new ones, repairs to all others as necessary, and all new hinges in February 1875. William Heath was allowed $100 for the job.[32] Repairs were necessary again in 1877 and again in 1881 when C.H. Sansbury and another man worked thirteen days repairing shutters and repairing and replacing hinges.[33] The *Fisherman and Farmer* report of the Grand Jury's findings in the spring of 1894 indicate that further repairs were again required. The report states that some of the shutters were "off and hanging in a dangerous condition."[34]

One other interesting addition to the courthouse was a gate put on the front door of the building in the summer of 1895. While the main doors had to be kept open during the hot summer months, the gate was to keep cattle and other animals out.[35]

Although there is no specific order recorded in either the Minutes of the old County Court or the Board of Commissioners Minutes, by the early 1870's the sheriff had a separate office of his own in the courthouse. This must have been the west office on the second floor of the building. The Commissioners issued an order in February 1875 for the Register's office, the Sheriff's office, stairway, and two rooms of the Clerk's office to be whitewashed.[36] It is likely that as the clerk's office was consolidated following the actions of 1868, the Superior Clerk took over both rooms on the East side of the building, forcing the sheriff upstairs. On other occasions throughout the period when the offices at the court were listed, each of the three officials was named individually as having a separate office. This occurred, for example, in the 1870's after a transition was made from wood to primarily coal burning stoves, and each of the offices received deliveries of coal. New stoves were bought for the Clerk's office in 1872 and 1886,[37] the Register's office in 1874,[38] and the Sheriff's office in 1877 and 1886.[39] The Courtroom received a new stove in December 1883.[40] Otherwise, the interior of the offices did not change in any appreciable way. An order was issued in February 1875 to "grain" two bookcases and the moulding around the edge of the floor in the Register's office.[41] The Commissioners also issued an order in February 1895 to replace the railing on the stairs leading to the second floor.[42]

The courtroom saw very few changes during these years. The Commissioners Minutes show that beginning with the January term of court in 1874 a carpet was laid over the stone floor of the courtroom during the winter (and possibly fall) sessions, and taken back up at the conclusion of each.[43] It is unclear whether this was a regular or an occasional practice. Some years a carpet is mentioned in the Minutes, other times it is not. The keeper of the courthouse, oftentimes the jailer and the individual hired to "wait on the court" while in session, was responsible for the carpet. In 1886, sacking was bought for the courthouse floor, and in 1891 fifty yards of the same material was bought "for the carpet in the courthouse."[44]

Benches were either made, repaired, or replaced at the courthouse at the end of 1890. A *Fisherman and Farmer* report of County expenses published on 9 January 1891 for the preceeding year simply lists "benches for the courthouse" among other expenditures reported by the jailer. A total of $80.25 was allowed for all of the items.[45] This is the only specific reference to benches at the courthouse since the substitution of chairs for the officials of the court in 1850. In all probability, the public continued to sit on benches of some kind during these years. The relation between the benches currently in the courthouse and those of an earlier period is unclear. It is clear, however, that unlike any other time in the building's history, chairs were being bought in quantities of a dozen or more at a time. Perhaps for the Assembly Hall, or for the offices, these chairs are described in 1872 only as "arm chairs."[46] After that, no description is given.

The first official thought given to changing the seating arrangement for the public in the courtroom was recorded in January 1895 when in response to a suggestion made by the Grand Jury, a committee was appointed to examine the possibility of putting in "elevated seats."[47] Commissioners Frank Wood and E.F. Waff returned the following month having concluded that because the available space was so small, it was "unwise" to install the seats.[48]

The first of several commemorative tablets was unveiled in the courtroom on 4 April 1892. Erected in memory of the "Honorable Judges of Edenton", the names which appeared on the tablet, as reported by the *Fisherman and Farmer* on 8 April were Christopher Gale, James Iredell Sr., James Iredell Jr., Augustus Moore, R.R. Heath, Thomas C. Manning, Edward W. Jones, Wm A. Moore, and Henry A. Gilliam.[49] It was placed in the rear apse of the courtroom near the chief magistrate's chair. John D. Cooper of Norfolk, Va. received the commission and executed the work.[50] Since 1892, four more names were added to the end of the list; Augustus M. Moore, William E. Bond, J. Wallace Winborne, and Richard Dillard Dixon. Curiously, the name of Samuel Johnston does not appear on the list reported by the newspaper, but preceeds Gale's name at the head of the tablet. Johnston, who chronologically came between Gale and Iredell was either written onto the tablet at a later date, perhaps snubbed by the powers that ran Edenton in

COMMEMORATIVE TABLET HONORING THE JUDGES OF EDENTON, UNVEILED IN THE COURTROOM ON 4 APRIL 1892

1892, or was a victim of mis-reporting on the part of the newspaper. A Justice of Chowan County during the prosperous late eighteenth century, Samuel Johnston was also a forebear of James C. Johnston who died in 1867 amid political and family controversy.

The list of groups and organizations known to have used the courthouse for private activities grew tremendously during these years. This increase can probably be attributed to the Commissioners' insistence that everybody obtain official permission before an available room (usually the Assembly Room, now more often called the Ballroom or Hall) could be used. The matter of charging fees, obtaining security deposits, etc. was changed, voted upon, decided, and changed again many times until 1887 when the Commissioners decided that a standard fee would always be charged to anyone wishing to use a room. The money collected was used to help maintain the building. Church meetings of all denominations and benefits for the poor were held at the courthouse, always at Christmas time. The Edenton Cornet Band practiced there. The Odd Fellows, Knights of Honor, and Ladies of the Moonlight were among the clubs that met there. Political organizations used the Hall as did the Hayes (Rutherford B.) and Wheeler Club prior to the 1876 election. The local militia used it as an armory until a more suitable place was found. Vocal recitals, educational exhibits, and a minstrel show were among the entertainments held there. Apparently someone tried to make lemonade and ice cream at the Hall during the summer of 1885 because the Commissioners prohibited this activity in July of that year.[51]

More official uses of the courthouse included the Board of Commissioners meeting. After 1879, they met in the courtroom unless cold weather or court business prevented it.[52] Presumably, one of the offices was used prior to 1879. As reported by the *Albemarle Enquirer* on 29 July 1886, the Democratic Convention of Chowan County was to be held at the courthouse to select delegates to the State and various District conventions.[53] The Town Council also met at the courthouse by September 1895, possibly before.[54] The County Board of Magistrates, an eleven member board which from 1875 to 1895 officially elected the Board of Commissioners, also met at the courthouse. Periodically the two Boards would meet in a joint session to discuss the County Tax levy, among other matters.

President Grover Cleveland came close to visiting Edenton during a fishing trip on 23 May 1897, but he remained on board the lighthouse steamer "Violet" during its four hour stay in Edenton harbor.[55] President James Monroe's visit in 1819 remains Edenton's only Presidential visit.

County Jail and Other Structures, 1868-1896

During this period the County Jail (fifty years old in 1875) was first found to be seriously inadequate. The problem was not seen in terms of neglected or overdue repairs, but rather as requiring substantial remodelling of the building with an eye already cast towards its eventual replacement. Before the end of 1896, it was clear to the County Commisssioners that there were better ways and means of keeping prisoners secure than those practiced at the

Chowan Jail.

The specifications for the job of repairing the jail as offered to contractors in September 1873 probably describe the interior of the jail much as it had been for years. The upstairs rooms were to be floored with heart lumber one and one half inches thick. The iron bars in the windows were to be securely confined in the wall. The jailer was to direct this work, and see that locks were properly put on the doors. All rotten beams were to be replaced. Downstairs, all flooring and sleepers which were not sufficient were to be replaced, also with good heart timbers. The east room was to be lined with seasoned heart oak planks, eight inches wide and two inches thick which were to be placed perpendicularly and attached to four horizontally running three inch by four inch heart oak timbers on each wall. These timbers thus encircled the room and were firmly secured in the walls at spaced intervals. The plank lining was to be secured to the floor and ceiling with three inch by four inch chamfered heart oak binding. Other repairs to be performed included replacing the upper floor window frames with sashes so that they corresponded to those downstairs, (apparently not done by 7 April 1887 when the order was repeated), repair of all brickwork as needed and repair or replacement of all "sewerage boxes" in the jail. These were to be built as before, and lined with zinc. There were other directions regarding the buying of pipes which apparently brought rainwater into the jail. The roof was also to be newly shingled. All rotten timbers were to be replaced. The roof of the piazza at the jailer's house was to be similarly refurbished. The shingles used were to be twenty-one inches by six inches by five-eighths inch, and of good cypress heart. Three months were allowed for the completion of the job.[56] A few changes in the specifications were made in the following month. (Three wall timbers six inches by two inches instead of four at three inches by four inches in the lower east room, shingles twenty-four inches long instead of twenty-one inches.) On 3 November C.E. Robinson offered his bond as contractor for the job. By 2 March 1874 Robinson's work was completed to the general satisfaction of the Committee of Commissioners. He was paid either a total of $680 or $544 (it is difficult to tell which) for the work specified by the contract, and $40 for other work included in the repairs.

Repairs were again required by May 1878.[57] An escape of more than one prisoner the previous October[58] may have had something to do with the need for these repairs. The following specifications amount to a rebuilding of the 'secure' lower east room, an iron cage being built into the existing room:

Flooring that is decayed to be removed and iron bars ½" thick and 1½" wide be crossed so as to leave space of 8" square to be firmly riveted together and to be firmly set beneath the flooring through the walling on the north side of the jail. The flooring then to be replaced by good heart lumber similar to that now there. Perpendicular bars of the same size of iron running from the top of said room and securely riveted at the top through the wall, the entire depth of the wall and at the flooring to elbow and run out of the floor 3 ft. to be securely confined by rivets or spikes to the flooring at their sd. elbow and along the end of sd. run. These bars to be set 10" inches apart and to extend around the four sides. Horizontal bars of the same size of iron to extend around the four sides of the jail. The bottom one to be at the angle of the perpendicular bars. Sd. bars to be 8" apart and placed horizontally to height of 7 ft. from the floor and at every point of contact with the perpendicular bars be firmly and securely riveted through the same.[59]

The contract was let on 1 June 1878, and the work was again to be completed in three months. Alf Moore, County Register and Clerk to the Board of Commissioners, was granted the contract with a low bid of $645. He submitted his bond in August. By October, Moore asked for an extension of the deadline for the iron work, and requested permission to proceed with the wood work.[60] He asked for another extension in late November,[61] and officially forfeited the contract on 2 December. He was paid $50 to cover his purchase of materials to that date. The Commissioners agreed to let out the contract once again, and then reconsidered.[62] On 7 January 1879, Sheriff M.C. Brinkley was ordered to repair the jail, making it secure at a cost no greater than $150.[63] Ten months later, he was allowed approximately $105 for repairing the jail.[64] There is no record of what work was performed, but it is clear that the iron work, as originally described, was not. Three months later, more repairs were ordered, and again relatively inexpensive repairs were performed.[65] This sequence repeated itself several times until 1885. The Building Committee which received R.N. Hines' repairs to the courthouse and minor repairs to the jail reported in June 1885 that the jail was still insecure, and would remain so "until rebuilt or remodelled."[66] Letters were sent to two different companies in November of that year requesting prices and information regarding steel jail cells.[67] At the same time, the Board of Commissioners agreed to let out work to make the jail secure against escape. Finally, on 11 June 1886, the Commissioners and Magistrates met in a joint session, and reached the following conclusion:

> . . . the object of this meeting being to consider the best means to secure the jail against escape therefrom of prisoners. . . it was ordered that whereas there are no funds at present, no funds in hand, and no lawful means of getting the funds within 12 months that the consideration of buying iron or steel cells be indefinitely postponed.[68]

The issue was raised again by the Board of Commissioners in March 1888 when again, because of the financial condition of the county, any extraordinary expense on the County Jail was considered "inexpedient."[69]

After the subject of steel cells was dropped, attention was turned towards the fence or wall built around the jail. The high wall which already stood on the south side of the jail was to be put in good order following the January 1888 meeting of the Commissioners.[70] The posts were to be of white or post oak. The following April, Theo Ralph was paid $125 for repairs to the jail, and for building a fence round the jail.[71] Although some work may have been done to the high wall, the fence referred to is probably the one which surrounded the entire complex of buildings on the Jail lot (as shown by a single solid line on the Sanborn Map of 1893 and is not another high wall enclosing the jail yard to the north of the building. That wall was built in the spring of 1892, when in the months of March and April, D.W. Raper was paid $9 for 720 feet of lumber "for the jail yard"; B.E. White, $67.50 for 45 days "carpenters work on Jail walls"; and W.H. Brown, $9.92 for oak lumber "for walls around the Jail."[72] R.H. Hall also received payment for tin work on the jail and jail walls.[73] Although much of this tin work went towards gutters for the building, later records show that the wooden fence was covered with tin, and then painted.[74] Iron and more tin were also used in repairing the jail door.[75]

The jail continued to be whitewashed both inside and out during this period. Stoves, apparently one on each floor, were periodically replaced. The rear stairs to the second floor were also repaired as necessary.

The Commissioners also either ordered or allowed several other changes at the jail lot. In September 1884, the Building Committee recommended that the cookroom or kitchen be rebuilt.[76] The job was presumably included within R.N. Hines' contract in 1885. The Sanborn map for that year shows the kitchen as a two story shingle roofed structure to the east of the jail along the edge of the lot. A well, mentioned for the first time and identified in the Commisssioners Minutes as "in the Jail yard" was cleaned and repaired in July 1883.[77] Jailer J.W. Spruill was allowed to build a dining room adjacent and to the rear of the jailer's house in January 1889.[78] He was to build it at his own expense, and would have the right to remove it at any time. This one story structure appears on the 1893 Sanborn map of Edenton, to the north and east of the dwelling.

Other changes in and around Edenton included the removal of the town's whipping post in July 1870.[79] The Market House, repaired by C.E. Robinson in October 1871 for $124,[80] in use until at least January 1892, was torn down in 1893. The *Fisherman and Farmer* reported on 14 April 1893 that a referendum had been held in town to determine whether a new market should be built. The negative vote won by a margin of 59 votes.[81] On 5 December of that year, the Town Council gave its permission to have the bricks of the Old Market sold.[82]

In March 1894, the Town Council received permission from the county to build a "truck and ladder house" on the lot near the jail.[83] The building is shown on the 1898 Sanborn map directly west of the jail. Edenton's Town Hall was to be put up for auction in December 1871, and by the following August David Lee was allowed to put up steps to the building "for his convenience."[84] Another town building, the Gun and Watch house, was rented in 1872, and then sold four years later.[85] It is also interesting to note that in 1870, David Lee was given permission to make bricks on one of the town commons in an area described as having boundaries "from Cemetary St. (parallel to and north of Hicks St.) on the south, to the County Rd., and from Granville St. 80 yards west."[86]

One of the most important events in Edenton history occurred on 19 December 1881 when the Norfolk and Southern Railroad opened its line to town.[87] Referenda supporting the extension of the N &S line to Edenton had been held in August 1877 and again in November 1878.[88]

CHOWAN COUNTY COURTHOUSE AND COURTHOUSE GREEN (reprinted courtesy of People's Bank, Edenton, N.C.)

CONTEMPORARY VIEW OF THE CHOWAN COUNTY COURTHOUSE

From Expansion
To Supersession
1896-1988

The Courthouse, 1896-Present

The first additions to the courthouse were built in August and September 1897. The St. Louis Art Metal Company was awarded the contract on 2 August 1897 to build two vaults, one on each side of the building, thus enlarging the offices of both the Register of Deeds and the Clerk of Court. By the terms of the contract, all work was to be done within 75 days from the date the contract was awarded. The county was to pay $2600 for the construction.[1] M.A. Hughes was to be superintendent for the project, but Theo Ralph was paid for this work in January 1898.[2] All work was completed on time, and the county officially received the vaults on 16 October 1897.[3] The final installment of the contracted price was paid in October 1900. Each vault adds approximately 90 square feet of floor space to its adjoining office. A single rear window in each addition was fitted on the inside with a steel shutter. Five course American bond was used in the outer brickwork. Simulated modillions are fashioned in the brick cornice which consists of the top three courses. Like the rest of the courthouse, the vaults were covered with tin roofs.

Another vault was built onto the courthouse, this time a single addition to the Register of Deeds office. Built between 1920 and 1927 as indicated by the Sanborn maps, the vault is not mentioned in the Commissioners Minutes until 6 December 1926. On that occasion the balance of the contract for building the vault, $805, was paid.[4] Adding approximately another 60 square feet to the Register's office directly behind the 1897 vault, this addition disrupts for the first time the balance of the building's symmetry. Unfortunately, newspapers of the time which may have reported on reaction to the vault, or given other pertinent details are not available.

The final addition to the courthouse, the boiler room and chimney built onto the rear of the courthouse did cause a bit of a stir among some Edenton residents. The Commissioners had decided that some kind of central heating system was a necessity at the courthouse. Plans for modernizing the heating plant were already underway in June 1947.[5] A system which could eventually accomodate a new jail, should the old one be replaced was to be among the requirements suggested by the Board. On 22 September 1947, local builder C.B. Mooney was awarded the contract to erect the building which would house the system on the back of the courthouse.[6] His bid of $2450 was offici-

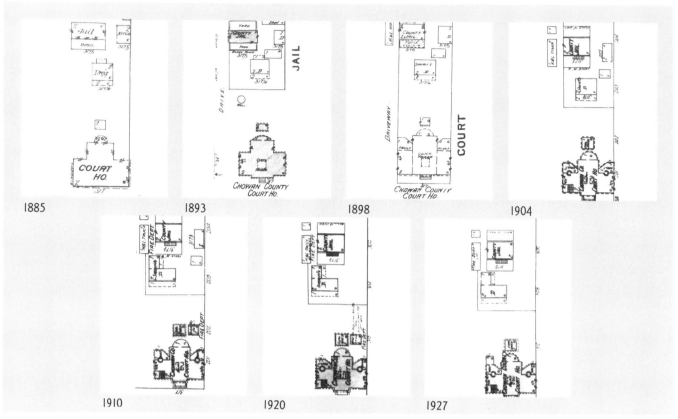

SANBORN MAP COMPANY MAPS OF THE COURTHOUSE LOTS. Reading from left to right: 1885, 1893, 1898, 1904, 1910, 1920, and 1927 (Reprinted by permission of Sanborn Map Company; Pelham, N.Y.)

ally accepted, while the contract providing the heating equipment itself was temporarily left open. This was due to a possible change in the plans regarding the Panelled Room.[7] The original specifications projected a total expenditure of $6955.[8] By 9 October, the foundation of the ten feet by fifteen feet boiler room was already in place, but construction was halted at some point before 20 October because of objections to the addition voiced by part of the Edenton community.[9] A special public meeting of the Board of Commissioners was held at the courthouse on 20 October to discuss these objections. At the meeting a petition was read which underscored the historic value of the building, commented upon the way in which the boiler room would "materially mar the beauty of the rear view of the courthouse," and suggested that a separate structure be located further away from the courthouse, particularly in view of its projected use in conjunction with future buildings.[10] Other suggestions brought up at the meeting included putting the heating units underground, under the courthouse, or in the coal shed. These were discussed and discounted as impossible or impractical, in any case offering no real alternative solution. Board Chairman W.W. Byrun defended the Commissioners against any charges of not wishing to preserve the courthouse. Chamber of Commerce President H.A. Campen suggested that if preserving the original shape of the courthouse was the issue, then the extensions already added on to the building should be taken down. He mentioned the western side view of the building which was made up of three distinct lines of masonry. A more 'central' location with respect to a future jail was dismissed because the county was not completely sure that a new jail was necessary. As the meeting went on, the issue became whether there should be a new heating system at the courthouse or not. E.W. Spires, Clerk of Court, reminded everyone that the Panelled Room was still heated by the fireplaces, and told several stories of near accidents which could have ended in disaster. The meeting ended with a decision to leave the matter in the hands of the Commissioners.[11] The boiler room and chimney were constructed as planned onto the rear of the courthouse to the east of the rear apse. The chimney rises approximately four feet above the courthouse roof line.

The contract for the oil burning heating system and its installation was awarded in early October to W. M. Wiggins and Co. of Wilson, North Carolina at a cost of $5295. A late change in the specifications for this system provided for the placement of radiators in the Panelled Room rather than overhead heating units as originally planned. The new heating plant was expected to be in operation by Christmas 1947. Architect Frank Benton, also of Wilson, acted as a consultant on the project.[12]

Work on the brickwork of the building included periodic painting until 1960. In June 1904, Dorsey Stewart received approximately $40 as partial payment for "painting the courthouse." Anderson Luten repaired brickwork at the building at the same time.[13] In July, John C. Bond was paid approximately $125 for paint, putty, varnish, and other materials used for "painting the courthouse." Also in July, Stewart and Anderson were paid an unstated sum for more of their work on the building[14] In August, Bond received another $27 and Stewart another $38.[15] In January 1900, The *Eastern Courier* suggested that "a coat of paint be put upon the outside of the building" to complement the work then being done inside the courthouse.[16] Photographic evidence also indicates that between 1910 and 1940 the color of the building was changed from white to red. According to the Commis-

BOILER ROOM AND CHIMNEY ADDED TO THE REAR OF THE COURTHOUSE IN 1947

EXTERIOR REAR VIEW OF THE COURTHOUSE

CHOWAN COUNTY COURTHOUSE
PAINTED RED WITH WHITE TRIM, CA.
1932 (North Carolina Division of Archives
and History, Raleigh, N.C.)

COURTHOUSE SURROUNDED BY
SCAFFOLDING IN PREPARATION FOR
THE REMOVAL OF YEARS OF PAINT,
AUGUST, 1960 (North Carolina Division of
Archives and History, Raleigh, N.C.)

sioners Minutes, the only extensive painting job done to the exterior of the
courthouse between these two dates took place in the fall of 1925. On 7
December of that year, C.S. Morgan received $668.49 for painting the court-
house and the roof of the jail.[17] The shutters were apparently removed from
the courthouse at the same time. The string course and the arches over the
windows were apparently always painted white in contrast to the red painted
brick. In 1960, however, the County Commissioners decided to remove the
paint from all of the building's exposed brickwork. On 1 August, the A. Lynn
Thomas Co. of Richmond Va. was awarded the contract to do the job.[18] A
test was made on a small section of the building on the 11th and 12th of the
month. By the 18th, the job was underway. Expected to take four to six weeks
to complete, the cost of the paint removal was $4500.[19] Apparently the
building was steam cleaned or blasted. Several people in Edenton maintain
that it was sand blasted.[20] The proceedure left the soft handmade bricks and
the old mortar of the courthouse severely damaged. The Commissioners met
in special session on 8 December to discuss the matter of repairing the
damage, and decided unanimously to go ahead with all necessary repairs.
Once again A. Lynn Thomas was granted the contract.[21] After receiving the
$4500 payment on 5 December for removing the paint[22], the company
received three other payments in March and April for work on the courthouse totalling $2904.51.[23]

COMMEMORATIVE TABLET INSCRIBED
WITH IMPORTANT DATES IN CHOWAN
COUNTY HISTORY PLACED IN THE
FRONT WALL OF THE COURTHOUSE
IN 1910

   The outer walls of the courthouse also received three commemorative
tablets during these years. An appropriation of $55 was set aside for the first
of these in April 1910. The inscription, having to do with Chowan County
history, the dates of the two County courthouses, etc., was submitted to the
Board by the Daughters of the American Revolution on 1 August 1910, and
approved by the Board upon verification of the information provided.[24] The
following month, the Commissioners ordered that the tablet be made with
plain lettering and no color. Set in the left (west) side of the building's facade

TABLET HONORING THE CHOWANOCK
INDIANS PLACED IN THE COURT-
HOUSE WALL IN 1912

NATIONAL HISTORIC LANDMARK SITE
MARKER PLACED IN FRONT OF THE
COURTHOUSE IN 1971

that autumn, the final cost of $60.17 was paid by the county on 2 January 1911.[25] Permission to erect a second tablet, corresponding to the first, was granted to the I.O.R.M. (Improved Order of Red Men) by the Commissioners in February 1912.[26] Honoring the Chowanock Indians, the tablet was placed in the right (east) side of the facade of the courthouse. In August 1916, the Daughters of the American Revolution petition requesting a plaque dedicated to the participants of the Edenton Tea Party was allowed by the Commissioners.[27] Made of bronze, the plaque is set in the courthouse wall, under the window directly to the left of the front door. Its unveiling was part of a program sponsored by the Daughters of the American Revolution which included the presentation of four markers around Edenton.[28] A fourth commemorative marker, not located on the courthouse, but on a stone immediately in front of it identifies the building as a National Historic Landmark, a distinction officially bestowed in July 1970.[29] Permission to mount the marker was granted by the Commissioners in April 1971.[30]

Throughout the first half of this period very little work was done to the roof of the courthouse. It was painted approximately every ten years, and received periodic and routine maintenance. One small repair which might be associated with general roof repair was the application of tin to the top of the pediment over the front doorway in August 1903.[31] In June 1939 Commissioners Warren, Boyce, and Dixon were instructed to examine the roof and report back to the Board.[32] As early as March 1938, the *Chowan Herald* reported that the courthouse would soon have a new roof.[33] A contract was awarded to W.M. Martin and Company of Richmond, Virginia in May 1940 to put a new roof on the building.[34] Work on the project had already begun by 25 July when the *Herald* reported that the new roof would be made of "Mohawk asbestos shingles of the kind used in the restoration of Williamsburg." [35] Two to three weeks was allowed for the completion of the job.

By 1954, this roof was no longer adequate, and the county sought bids on a contract to replace it. A.L. Perry's proposal was accepted in February 1954. He was to furnish and install a "300# asphalt shingle roof with 30# felt, using inch and a half nails. . . furnish and install four copper valleys. . . replace any rotten sheathing which may be found, and point up any cracks in the two chimneys." [36] A month later, he received $1064 for the job.[37] In July 1960, Perry received another $435 for working on the roof.[38]

In the late 1970's, the County decided not only to replace the asphalt shingle roof, but to restore the roof to a condition appropriate to its mid-eighteenth century origin. The North Carolina Department of Cultural Resources accepted the County's initial application for a Heritage Conservation and Recreation Service grant in October 1978.[39] Estimates of the cost of the project ranged from $30,000 to $40,000. In November, the County contracted J. Everette Fauber of Lynchburg, Va. to provide Architectural services in conjunction with the restoration of the roof.[40] Much of the next year was spent determining the proper materials, particularly the type of shingle which would be used. In September 1979, assurances were made by the County to Cultural Resources that over $20,000 had been set aside as matching funds to the available grants.[41] Work began in the fall of 1980 and

was completed before 1 January 1981. The total expenditure was $39,846.[42] The shingle finally used was a red cedar shake.

The cupola and the clock within it were changed in two major ways during these years. The first, the installation of the metal louvres in the arches of the upper stage cannot be exactly dated. It occurred sometime between 1910 and 1940, probably earlier rather than later. A reading of the Commissioners Minutes suggests that J.H. Bell, whose trade in tin and sheet iron work had included work on the gutters and roof of the courthouse, may have performed this job in May or June 1913. On 2 June he was paid for "work and material on the Cupola."[43] The other change can be dated exactly. A contract for the electrification of the courthouse clock was granted to Clock Service of Kendall, Florida on 7 August 1950.[44] The cost to repair and electrify the clock was $700. A newspaper article from 10 August reported on the worn condition of the mechanism and the uncertain strength of the cables which held weights of 1000 and 700 pounds. The article also relayed a story that on an occasion approximately 40 years before, these weights broke from the cables and crashed down through the floor.[45] This story has not been either conclusively confirmed or denied. By 1959, the clock was being maintained by Campen's Jewlery Service of Edenton.[46]

Other minor repairs and maintenance work on the cupola included regular painting. At times the pediment around the clock face was painted white, at other times, a dark color. The clock face itself was painted in April 1930.[47] The Town of Edenton, always sharing responsibility with the County for the cupola as it related to the clock, was first given permission to wire and light the clock tower, at its own expense, in July 1915.[48] The question of whether the clock should strike the hour on a twenty-four hour basis was referred to the Town Council in December 1943.[49] For some time during the war, the clock was quiet from 10 PM until 7 AM.[50]

The way in which the doors of the courthouse opened was ordered changed in 1910. Probably for greater safety in case of fire, and in compliance with proper building codes, the doors were to open towards the outside.[51] In May 1924, the doors were (again ?) re-hung.[52]

Many of the modifications that effected the courthouse as a whole as it has moved through the twentieth century had to do with technological innovations. The Masons were the first to bring electric lights into the building. In August 1904, the commissioners gave them permission to light their Hall and to put a light at the head of the stairway leading to the second floor.[53] Commissioner Frank Ward was authorized in January 1907 to arrange for the wiring and fitting of the building with lights.[54] During May, June, and July of that year, about $1000 was spent to complete the job. The commissioners ordered the Sheriff in September 1907 to have the chandelier (in the courtroom?) to be fitted with "electric globes" before the next session of court.[55] Repairs to the wiring included work in the vicinity of the Masonic Hall in late July 1940.[56] R.J. Boyce was awarded a contract to rewire the entire building in December 1954.[57] Air conditioning made its first appearance at the courthouse in 1958 when four window units were purchased, and the necessary wiring was added.[58]

Interior plumbing was another twentieth century improvement, completed at the courthouse by December 1925. C.L. Russ did the work for $567.[59] This was the first full plumbing system installed at the building. The bathrooms which are currently in the hall beneath the stairway were installed in

CHOWAN COUNTY COURTHOUSE AND FOUNTAIN ON THE GREEN, CA. 1904-1910 (reprinted courtesy of Rebecca Warren)

early 1959 by the Edenton Construction Company.[60]

Wall and floor coverings also changed during these years. These will be looked at in more detail as the various rooms of the building are examined. Generally speaking, surfaces which had been whitewashed up until this time were first painted in 1911-1912. Wall papering, introduced to selected areas as early as 1909, was used to a greater degree in December 1925.[61] Put up by H.A. Hobbs, the paper was apparently replaced and painted over on several occasions. Although the records do not specify any further use of wall paper after 1925, the building was extensively replastered by A.N. Bateman in 1949 at a cost of $725, and therefore must have been repapered in certain areas since then.[62] One of the more special occasions for which the interior of the courthouse was repainted and generally cleaned and repaired was the celebration in 1932 surrounding the dedication of the Joseph Hewes monument. Authorized by an Act of Congress, the monument stands near the foot of the courthouse green.

One of the most significant changes to occur inside the courthouse during its entire history took place just at the turn of the century. After the first initiative to change the seating arrangement in the courtroom had failed in 1895, Commissioner Frank Wood was appointed to investigate the situation again in November 1899.[63] Six months later, Theo Ralph, the local builder often employed by the county, was paid $224 for work done to the courtroom and the courthouse "steeple."[64] Although the nature of the work is not described, it is most likely that the raised wooden platform was built in the courtroom at this time. In the first section of his *Historical and Genealogical Register*, J.R.B. Hathaway commented in passing on the Chowan County courthouse, "with its stone floor."[65] Also, on 25 January 1900, the Edenton newspaper *Eastern Courier* reported, "We are glad to note the fact that work on the interior of the courtroom had begun."[66] The lack of any comparable expense designated for the courtroom, the choice of the craftsman employed, the size of the expenditure itself, and the fact that the stone floor seems to be beyond the memory of folks alive today, all point towards this conclusion.

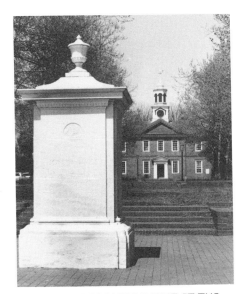

JOSEPH HEWES MONUMENT AT THE SOUTH END OF THE COURTHOUSE GREEN, ERECTED IN 1932

JURY AREA ON THE WEST SIDE OF THE COURTROOM

TABLET HONORING WILLIAM SKINNER, CLERK OF COURT, WHICH HANGS NEAR THE BAR ON THE EAST SIDE OF THE COURTROOM. The tablet fails to mention the brief tenure of Charles E. Robinson as Clerk of the newly constituted Court from April to October 1868

The 'picket fence' which surrounds the platform and helps to minimize the disturbing effect of traffic on its way to and from the offices while court is in session were probably also built at this time. The platform for the jury apparently was not. An October 1925 order from the commissioners appointed J.T. Satterfield and John G. Wood to look after "building a platform in the jury box."[67] Listed as one of several repairs to be done at the courthouse, it is unclear whether the platform replaced an earlier one, or was itself an addition to the courtroom. The arrangement of the jury box changed in February 1940 when new swivel chairs with arm rests were installed.[68] The new chairs were larger than the ones previously used, and could not all fit across the two tiers of the jury box. As a result, the current arrangement with two of the twelve chairs placed at floor level was adopted.

Other work involving the flooring in the courtroom included the replacement of the floor in the Bar, ordered in September 1909.[69] In November 1949, Superior Judge Nimocks praised the attractive appearance of the courthouse, specifically mentioning the "attractive flooring placed in the courtroom."[70] The Commissioners Minutes show that Quinn Furniture had just put congoleum and tile asphalt in the courthouse and the offices.[71] It is likely that the Attorney's area, and possibly the Judge's Bar, all now carpeted, received this covering. The jury box may also have been involved, as there is an accompanying expense for reinstalling the juror's seats.[72] Carpeting in the courtroom was first ordered by the Commissioners in May 1968.

As has already been indicated, the walls of the courtroom were first painted in 1912.[73] The plaster on the walls and ceiling was periodically repaired, or done over completely. In September 1931, the Commissioners granted W.S. Summerall permission to place a marble tablet in the courtroom honoring the memory of his grandfather, W.R. Skinner.[74] Skinner was Clerk of Court (first the County Court and then the new Superior Court) from 1849 to 1885, with the exception of the months August to October 1868. The plaque hangs near the Bar on the side of the room closest to the Clerk's office.

Until 1947, heat in the courtroom was provided by a stove which sat towards the front, next to the shortened row of benches on the right side of the room. After 1947, radiators which were part of the newly installed heating system did the job. A proposal to enclose and air condition the courtroom was brought up to the Commissioners in March 1970.[75] This would have solved the problem of noise coming from people on their way to the offices in the building during court, as well as cooled the room. In July of that year, Wilson architect Atwood Skinner was asked to investigate this possibility and determine if it could be done without "detracting from the historical structure."[76] The idea was dropped.

The upstairs office on the west side of the building continued to house several different officials and agencies during these years. It was still the sheriff's office at the turn of the century. Repairs were made to the area around the hearth in that office during the winter of 1906-07 to keep it from sagging.[77] A safety warning was also issued by the Commissioners not to have two stoves (one in the Sheriff's office, the other in the Register's office) over one another and vented out the same chimney. On 4 February 1924, the

Commissioners ordered the office cleared and made ready to accomodate the County (Demonstration) Agent, N.K. Rowell.[78] The first reference to this official position occurs in the Minutes of the Board for February 1919.[79] It is unclear where the sheriff's office was moved, but by January 1925 rent was paid for an office to be used by the sheriff.[80] After July 1927, this money was paid to the Bank of Edenton.[81] By August 1937, the Commissioners Minutes refer to the room as the "old Sheriff's office", and indications are that the County Agent was no longer there.[82] The Farm Security Administration office was moved into the room by 24 February 1938.[83] An article in the *Chowan Herald* on that day said that the room was to be heated with steam heat furnished from a small furnace in the Register of Deeds office.[84] The installation of that furnace had been completed and paid for on 1 February 1937 at a cost of $275.[85] The newspaper went on to say that a fire-proof covering was to be put on the floor. After the Farm Security Administration office was closed, and at least by 9 October 1947, the room became the County Tax Supervisor's office.[86] Empty for some years after the tax supervisor moved, the room served exclusively as a jury room. As was the case with the rest of the courthouse, after 1947, the office was heated with radiators from the central heating system.

The Masonic Hall on the east side of the second floor experienced its first major change, at least insofar as it pertained to official interest, when after more than 175 years, and some years after extensive renovations to the Hall by the Lodge in the summer of 1940[87] the Masons left the courthouse. Their new building opened in 1954. In November 1966, the Clerk of Court was authorized to expand into the old Masonic Hall, and to install an intercom between the two floors.[88] The following July, the Clerk requested a conveyor be installed between the two floors for greater ease in transporting documents.[89] The Park Manufacturing Company was paid $710 in December

MASONIC HALL OF THE UNANIMITY LODGE #7 IN THE EAST ROOM OF THE SECOND FLOOR OF THE COURTHOUSE (Reprinted by permission of Chowan County Unanimity Lodge #7)

ASSEMBLY HALL OF THE CHOWAN
COUNTY COURTHOUSE

1967 for installing a dumbwaiter.[90]

Unfortunately, there is a lack of information, particularly early information regarding the Panelled Room, Assembly Hall, Ballroom, or simply the
Hall in the courthouse. Few details prior to the twentieth century except for
instances of who used the room, and for what purpose have been uncovered.
From a documentary standpoint, the matter of whether or when the room
was painted prior to this time remains unclear. However, details regarding the
maintenance of the room during this century are available. A payment issued
for "papering the Courthouse Hall" in March 1909 may refer to the ceiling of
the room which was patched just prior to this date.[91] The same order which
refered to "building a platform in the Jury box" in October 1925 also listed
"papering overhead upstairs in the main part" among the necessary repairs.[92]
A committee was formed in July 1941 to recommend repairs for the Hall.[93]
The committee reported the floors to be in bad shape, and that the walls,
painted last in 1932, needed new paint. Work on the fireplaces was needed,
and a better way to heat the room was necessary. Finally, they suggested that
the room be furnished "appropriately", and that portraits of early Edentonians
be found and placed there.[94] C.B. Mooney was granted the contract to repair
the room. The renovations, completed by October 1943, were noted in the
Chowan Herald, and described as a "splendid improvement."[95] Portraits of
Joseph Hewes and Hugh Williamson, donated by the Hewes family and Mrs.
James Webb respectively were accepted in April 1946.[96] In June of that year,
$600 was set aside by the county for the care of the room. It was sanded and
refinished in November and December 1949 by A.E. Lassiter, who again
worked refinishing the floor in April 1953.[97] The painting of Queen Anne
which hangs in the room was contributed by Mr. and Mrs. John G. Fletcher
It was accepted by the county in August 1952.[98]

The offices of the Clerk of Court and the Register of Deeds were both
repaired and modernized in a similar manner throughout the years. Protect-
ing records and documents from fire continued to be a most important
priority. The addition of the vaults themselves was an essential step towards

PORTRAIT OF JOSEPH HEWES, PLACED
IN THE ASSEMBLY HALL IN APRIL 1946

this end, while the substitution of metal cabinets and counters for wooden ones was also important. Beginning with the initial installation of metal files in the new vaults in 1897, the process continued until September 1911 when all the wooden cabinets in the Clerk's office were pulled, sold at auction, and replaced with metal.[99] Also during the summer of 1911 at the direction of Commissioner Frank Wood, that office was fitted with iron and steel costing $282 from Dietrich Brothers, and metal doors from Dahlstrom Metalic Door Company.[100] Both offices received steel counters with roller shelves and document files in the spring of 1949.[101] Fireproof insulation was added to the ceiling of the rear vault of the Register's office in 1954.[102]

PORTRAIT OF HUGH WILLIAMSON, PLACED IN THE ASSEMLY HALL IN APRIL 1946

The offices also had to be protected against water damage. In the early months of 1938, the vaults on both sides of the building were renovated to protect their contents from an increasingly serious problem of dampness and mildew. As reported in February 1938 by the *Chowan Herald*, these renovations would include the application of a new waterproof plaster and the insertion of ventilators in the floors to increase the circulation of air. Apparently the condition of the walls behind the filing cabinets in the clerk's office, exposed by the Clerk, R.D. Dixon, persuaded the Commissioners to take action.[103] In all likelihood, the work was done by Norris and Batton who received $428 for unspecified work at the courthouse on 7 March 1938.[104]

Other twentieth century innovations in the offices included the introduction of linoleum, ordered for the floors of the Register's office in January 1907, and the Clerk's office two months later.[105] Carpets were often put on top of the linoleum. A telephone was authorized for the Clerk's office in February 1921, while the Register's office did not get its phone until January 1942.[106] Prior to 1947, a stove still supplied the heat to the clerk's office. This was also the case in the Register's office until early 1937. At that time a small furnace was installed. Both offices were equipped with radiators after 1947. Extremes of temperature, both hot and cold, were not unusual in the vaults. Top coats sometimes had to be worn inside during the winter. Until the addition of air conditioning, fans were used to help relieve the summer heat.[107] There are references to screen doors at the entrances to the offices in the 1930's.

The transcribing of records in use at the courthouse continued. The Register's Books, for example, were ordered to be recopied beginning in May 1933.[108] The task of indexing papers in the Register's and Clerk's offices was authorized in October 1946 and completed before April 1949 by the Felgar Indexing Company.[109] Efforts to preserve old records accelerated during these years, sometimes setting the County and the North Carolina Historical Commission (the predecessor of the Division of Archives and History) at odds over proceedure and rights of possession. In August 1913, County Commissioner F.W. Hobbs was instructed to go through the old books and papers in the courthouse and destroy all that were of no use.[110] There is no telling what may have been lost on that occasion. Within four years the Commissioners issued an order to have the old records sorted and preserved.[111] Some were sent to Raleigh for this purpose in July 1919, more were loaned to the North Carolina Historical Commission in May 1921.[112] Other papers kept "upstairs" at the courthouse were examined in early 1927. Those considered to be of use were to be put in the Register's vault.[113] By the late 1930's, if not before, appeals from the Historical Commission for the county to hand over many of its old documents were being denied.[114] Meanwhile, available storage space at the courthouse continued to shrink. All tax scrolls prior to 1935 were moved from the Register's vault to a building behind the jail in 1940.[115] An unexpected discovery also occurred in that year when many old papers were found in the Masonic Hall under the Master's steps which were then being replaced.[116] A collection of old documents stored in the People's Bank and Trust Building was examined in November 1958. These turned out to be the records of the eighteenth century General Court.[117] In September 1961, the county released its historical documents to the N.C. Division of Archives and History.[118] Three months later, eighteeth century volumes of the *Laws of the United States* which had been stored in the documents closet of the Register's office were also sent to Raleigh to be preserved and then returned.[119] One other interesting incident involving old county documents occured in February 1965 when a building behind the county office building was being destroyed to make room for a parking lot. As the *Chowan Herald* reported on the 25 February, Grayson Harding and Robert B. Smith rescued five boxes of old papers before the trash trucks came to get them. It is unclear if other documents were destroyed.[120]

Various community activities of the kind that had always been held at the courthouse continued to be held there. Other activities included the use of the Hall by the Red Cross during the flu epidemic of 1918.[121] Also, in August 1942, the second floor of the building was offered to the engineers and architects who were constructing the nearby Marine Glider Base.[122] The County Board of Commissioners continued to meet in the courthouse during these years. Prior to 1935-40 they met in the Register's office. After that, a table at the front right hand side of the courthouse was used. As always, the Register of Deeds served as Clerk to the Board.

In June 1947, the County Building Committee met to evaluate the sufficiency of the County Buildings.[123] The report of the committee stated that the administrative needs of the county were being met by the courthouse. By 1968, eight years after the Hotel Joseph Hewes was bought by the county to be converted into offices, the days of the courthouse as the sole judicial building in the county were numbered. In March of that year, Superior Court Judge Albert Cowper called the courthouse "completely inadequate", and said that it should be turned into a museum.[124] The Grand Jury reported that the Register of Deeds required more space.[125] Judge Hubbard, also of the Superior Court met with the chairman of the Board of Commissioners in April 1970 to discuss plans for a new courthouse.[126] A special session of the Board was convened in June to discuss the same subject.[127] The Third Chowan County Courthouse was built a few blocks north of the Old Courthouse in 1978 and 1979. It was officially dedicated on 18 November 1979. The Second Chowan County Courthouse currently houses several county offices. It is also the site of District Court on those occasions when Superior Court is also being held in town. It still offers a most beautiful view of the Bay.

VIEW OF THE BAY FROM THE
ASSEMBLY HALL

CHOWAN COUNTY COURTHOUSE
WITH THE CONFEDERATE MONUMENT
IN PLACE ON THE COURTHOUSE
GREEN, CA. 1930's (North Carolina
Division of Archives and History,
Raleigh, N.C.)

CONFEDERATE MONUMENT AT ITS
PRESENT LOCATION AT THE END OF
MAIN STREET

County Jail and Other Structures, 1896-Present

Most, if not all of the miscellaneous structures that we have been concerned with up to this point were removed by 1897. Most of the structures that shall be discussed in this section are related to the jail in that they are either located near the jail, or are actually auxilliary buildings to it. The one structure of interest that does not fit either of these descriptions is the Confederate Monument. Erected and dedicated on 3 June 1904, the monument stood at the north end of the courthouse green facing the courthouse. At the ceremony marking the occasion a small tin box containing a list of confederate veterans living in Chowan County at the time and a copy of the *Edenton Transcript* from 27 May 1904 was buried at the site.[128] Beginning in late 1959, the Women's Club tried to obtain permission from the town to move the monument as part of a project to restore and beautify the green. For a year and a half a controversy surrounded this proposal. During this time, a town referendum on the issue was called for May 1960 and then cancelled. The local chapter of the Daughters of the Confederacy fought against moving the monument until the Women's Club withdrew its proposal citing its reluctance to enter "partisan politics", and the irrelevance of a non-binding referendum.[129] By 18 May 1961, the Commissioners accepted the proposal of the Women's Club which had been re-submitted with the stipulation that no county funds would be used for the project.[130] On 1 June 1961, the monument was moved to its current location at the end of Broad Street. The tin box buried 57 years earlier was found and opened on that occasion.[131]

The earliest and most major change to occur on the jail lot was the removal of the old Jailer's house and its replacement with a new dwelling on virtually the same site. In August 1905, the Commissioners awarded the contract for the construction of the new brick building to Miles Brown of Edenton on a bid of $2050. The house was wired in October by L.C. Moore. Construction was completed by 18 December when Brown received the balance due on the contract.[133] The rear ell on the house, or at least part of it was used as a cookroom for the jail, making the old kitchen on the jail lot superfluous. Permission to bring down the kitchen was granted in 1907, although it apparently was left standing until sometime between 1910 and 1920. The dining room which had been built adjacent to the old Jailer's house was also left standing until sometime during that decade. According to the Sanborn maps, the town built a hose house for the fire company on the courthouse lot just east of the coal shed between 1904 and 1910. Curiously, the Commissioners Minutes for February 1921 record the town receiving permission to move a hose house and put it between the coal house and the courthouse.[134] The small structure, smaller than the coal shed, appears on the maps of 1910 and 1920, but is gone by 1927. The only other building put up on the jail lot was a garage built for use by the Demonstration (County) Agents in February 1919. It measured sixteen feet by twenty feet and was located in the northeast corner of the lot.[135] All of the area around the jail was altered in the mid 1960's when it was turned into a parking lot. It is interesting to note that in 1952 the area behind the jail was suggested as a possible site for the Penelope

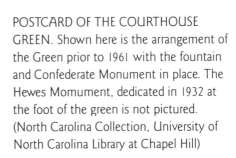

POSTCARD OF THE COURTHOUSE GREEN. Shown here is the arrangement of the Green prior to 1961 with the fountain and Confederate Monument in place. The Hewes Momument, dedicated in 1932 at the foot of the green is not pictured. (North Carolina Collection, University of North Carolina Library at Chapel Hill)

Barker house. The Commissioners denied the request.[136]

The county jail entered the twentieth century as it had left the nineteenth, outdated. On 10 July 1905, the Commissioners decided that an improvement at the jail was necessary:

> Whereas the present jail of Chowan County is unsafe, insufficient, and out of repair and more approved facilities for holding criminals has long been felt a a grave public necessity and whereas the judges and Board of Charities have from time to time recommended that the present jail be improved and repaired to such the needs of the County, the Board of Commissioners declare the said improvements to the County Jail a necessary expense to the County and a public necessity.

> Be it resolved that the County Jail be remodelled and equipped with steel cells and other approved appliances and equipment for the care of prisoners which will not exceed $3800 . . . .[137]

The Pauly Jail Building Company of St. Louis got the contract with a bid of $3800. The cells arrived in November 1905, and were installed on the lower floor of the remodelled building. They were examined, tested, and then officially received on 18 December.[138] During the renovations, prisoners were sent to Pasquotank County Jail.

After the introduction of these cells, the interior of the building changed very little. Iron bedsteads replaced wooden sleepers. An order to paint the inside of the jail in 1913 was followed on several occasions by others ordering the cells to be painted. Instructions to simply "whitewash the jail" occur until 1924. An order to paint the cells and have the second floor whitewashed was

JAILER'S HOUSE SITUATED BETWEEN THE COURTHOUSE AND THE JAIL

issued in 1941.[139] The windows in the second story, an area for less dangerous prisoners, were fitted with heavy wire netting in 1951.[140] A heater was purchased for the jail in November 1935, and replaced with a "new oil heater" in 1952.[141] A new heating system was installed by Joe Conger in 1967.[142] An order to have the Jail properly "piped to get water" was issued in June 1904.[143] A bid by Floars Electric and Plumbing to install "three new toilets in the lower level of the jail" was accepted by the County in August 1939.[144] In 1970, The Raleigh *News and Observer* described the jail as capable of holding 22 prisoners, with the women kept upstairs in "two dormitory like rooms" and the men downstairs in cells.[145]

The question of when the exterior of the jail was first painted is, as in the case of the courthouse, difficult to determine. The Commisioners issued orders in July 1877 to have the jail whitewashed "inside and out", and in August 1913 to specifically have the inside of the jail painted. On the latter occasion, L.C. Burton received about $14 for his work. The first reference to the use of paint at the jail occurs in June 1906 when Commissioners Wood and Byrum were instructed to determine the cost of painting the jail.[146] In October of that year E.B.F. Jones was awarded the contract to paint the jail for $24. Two coats of paint were specified.[147] Again, there is simply not enough information to make a conclusive statement.

Aside from the matter of paint, the jail's old shingle roof was removed, necessary repairs to the woodwork underneath were completed, and a new galvanized sheet iron roof was put on in November 1910. J.H. Bell received about $68 for covering the jail.[148] The roof was painted periodically. The windows in the back of the jail were ordered to be "double ironed and cemented up" in August 1913. They were ordered put back in February 1918 and again in November of that year.[149]

The brick walls which currently surround the jail were built in 1912, replacing the tall wooden fences which had previously stood there. Expenses for the "jail wall" are listed in the Commissioners Minutes for 1 April 1912. They include charges for materials from M.G. Brown (he built the brick Jailer's house) and a total of $356 for labor to J.H.Bell and (including his commission) F. Muth.[150] One interesting feature of these walls is the glass stuck in the top, placed there to discourage would-be escapees.

Serious consideration was again given to the idea of either enlarging or rebuilding the County Jail by 1942. In May 1945, Architect Frank Benton was requested to draw up plans for a new building, and submit them along with an estimate of the cost of construction.[151] In June, he was authorized to "proceed with his specifications" for the building of a new jail together with a heating system for the jail, jailer's house and the courthouse.[152] Although plans were apparently progressing, the County Building Program Committee reported in June 1947 that a new jail was not necessary, that the old one was only very rarely overcrowded, and could take care of the few number of prisoners who were usually in the County's custody.[153] The plans were dropped until 1958 when the Commissioners accepted Mr. Benton's contract for the "drawing of Plans and Specifications of a new office building and jail." The Board went so far as to order $3800 paid, to be credited against the cost of any building "should they ever be built."[154] The county's purchase of the Hotel Joseph Hewes as office space in 1960 solved one problem, and plans for the jail were again shelved.[155] In October 1967, the Commissioners were again considering a new jail.[156] Two years later, a State Jail Inspector pointed out the fire hazard created by the wooden rafters, the lack of a sprinkler system, and the absence of proper and separate facilities for men and women, or for first offenders. At the same time, the Board received a letter from Perquimans County requesting Chowan's adoption of a resolution which called for a District Jail. Chowan turned the suggestion down.[157]

The beginning of the end for Edenton's 1825 jail came in July 1970 when the Board of Commissioners met in special session with Clifton Craig of the State Department of Social Services.[158] Craig threatened to close the jail unless positive steps were taken to "provide an acceptable facility for the confinement of Chowan County prisoners." Renovations to the present structure or participation in a Regional Jail were given as alternatives. [159] The County clearly wanted to go on operating the jail. In October, representatives from North Carolina Social Services delivered an ultimatum to Chowan County insisting that "positive improvements" be taken or the jail would be closed in 30 days.[160] Several actions were suggested as "positive improvements" including the abandonment of the second floor and renovation of the first. But over the course of the next few years, the jail remained open as Chowan moved towards participation in a regional jail. Finally, the Jail in Edenton was closed, and Chowan County began shared operations at the Tri-County Jail on 1 July 1980.

FRONT WINDOWS OF THE COURT-HOUSE FROM THE ASSEMBLY HALL.

Conclusions:
Mysteries Remain

After all has been said and done, at least on this occasion, several mysteries regarding the Chowan County courthouse remain. But aside from questions regarding paint, or a roof in 1840, or interior columns in 1817, one set of overriding questions are especially nagging. Who built the courthouse? Who designed it? Why have no records documenting its construction been found? What about John Hawks?

Educated guesses can be made towards identifying craftsmen who may have worked on the courthouse. Gilbert Leigh and John Green are likely possibilities. Perhaps some of the woodworkers engaged at St. Paul's also contributed their talents to the courthouse. Skilled black craftsmen may have worked there.

But who designed the building? Much speculation has focused on John Hawks. A few of the familiar details of his life include his coming to North Carolina in 1764 in the company of then Lieutenant Governor Tryon. On 9 January 1767, the year the courthouse was begun, he contracted with Governor Tryon to build the Governor's Residence in New Bern. The building was to be finished in three years. Hawks spent much of the spring and summer of 1767 assembling materials and hiring skilled workmen for the project. On 4 June of that year the commissioners in Edenton advertised for a builder of their brick courthouse, and specifically said that the plan of the building, presumably complete, would be furnished. The first bricks at 'Tryon's Palace were laid on 26 August 1767. On 7 March 1768, Tryon wrote, ". . . the body of the house is already carried up to the Plate, in six weeks I expect to have the roof on it."[1] Meanwhile, on 22 December 1767, Hawks was rewarded with the profitable post of Collector at the Port of New Bern. Work at the "Palace" was completed and the house was opened in December 1770.

We know that Hawks drew a cupola for "the Edenton Church" in November 1769. In his *Architecture of the Old South*, Mills Lane states that Hawks "designed improvements to Edenton's public market, a two story brick structure like many typical 18th century English Town Halls, with an open arcade at the ground floors."[2] Unfortunately, Lane does not give a firm reference for this statement, and we are left wondering both about Hawks and the description of the market house. Hawks did, of course, design a prison for Edenton in June 1773. Although one may wonder whether a man of Hawks' ability would be asked to design the prison for Edenton and not the courthouse, the fact is that in 1773 an act was passed by the legislature specifically calling once again for a new prison in Edenton. The two buildings were originally linked in the Act of 1766, but as has been noted, only the prison remained to be built. Hawks may have submitted a design for it without having been involved with the courthouse. His letter to Joseph Hewes in October 1773, may have been equally, or more related to Hewes' position in the legislature than his status as a citizen of Edenton. Although it is very clear that Hawks did have many connections with Edenton, and that he may well have been the right man in the right place at the right time, this offers no proof of his connection with the courthouse. Finally, the notice in the *State Gazette* of 12 November 1790 which announced John Hawks' death does not mention The Chowan County Courthouse, but neither does it speak of anything except the fact of his death.[3] There is no word whatever regarding accomplishments, buildings, or positions. Like so many 'clues of ommission' turned up in this study, this bit of information seems as if it should be helpful, but is more tantalizing than solid. On one hand, 18th and early 19th century Edenton newspapers did not seem to report their own news in much detail. (For example, President Monroe's visit in 1819.) On the other hand, considering the prominence of the building in question, it is hard to imagine that a local editor's memory would have proved to be so short.

Where are the records for the courthouse? Not where anyone has yet looked. Perhaps in someone's attic or ashes. Consider the capricious and circuitous paths oftentimes taken by historical documents; by Hawks' drawing of the prison; and the connection between it, Ebenezer Paine, and the jail constructed in Edenton some fifty years later; or of the rescue of papers from a waiting garbage truck. Still, it is hard to imagine that a building such as the Chowan County Courthouse could have appeared with little more than a trace. We are then left without these answers, but with a most beautiful building which continues to excite our appreciation, and extend a tradition, even while it gently irks our curiosity.

VIEW OF THE GREEN AND BAY FROM THE FRONT OF THE COURTHOUSE.

Appendix A:
The Legislative Papers

Index to the Legislative Papers

The Legislative Papers

From SR 23 pp. 94-96, 1715

An Act for the Confirmation of the Laws passed this Session of Assembly & for repealing all former Laws not herein particulary Excepted.

I. Whereas in pursuance of an Act of Assembly made & ratified the 6th day of November last past the ancient standing laws of this Government have been carefully revised.

VI. And Be It Further Enacted by the Authority aforesaid that these following Laws shall be, remain, and continue, and they are hereby revived & continued.

IX. An Act to promote the building a Court house to hold the Assembly in, at the fork of Queen Ann's Creek commonly called Matchacamak Creek in Chowan precinct.

SR 25 p. 168, 1720

An Act in Additon to the Act for Making a Town at Queen Ann's Creek.

Whereas, one hundred Acres of Land lying in the Fork of Queen Ann's Creek was formerly granted by Tho's Peterson and Nath. Chevin, Esq'rs, for a Town, and two Acres thereof assigned for a Church, Court House and other publick Uses, the remainder was to be laid out into half acre Lots and the said Tho. Peterson and Nath. Chevin, Esq'rs, as Trustees, were impowered by the said Act for making a Town to assign and transfer the Said Lotts to such persons as would take them up and build on them in Such Time and according to Demension in the Said Act limited, but the said Tho. Peterson and Nath. Chevin being both now dead and there remains great part of the hundred acres not yet allotted, and no person being impowered to lay out and grand Lotts it hinders the Increase of the Said Town, wherefore for promoting the Said Town We pray that it may be Enacted, and

I. Be it Enacted by his Excellency the palatin and the rest of the true and absolute Lords Prop'ts of Carolina, by and with the Advice and Consent of the Rest of the Members of the General Assembly now met at the General Court House at Queen Anne's Creek in Chowan precinct for the N'o. East Part of the Said province, and by the Authority of the Same it is hereby Enacted, that the Remains of the Said hundred Acres not allotted, granted and the Condition fulfilled shall be vested in Daniel Richardson, Esq'r, as Trustee, who is hereby impowered by himself, his Assigns or Attorney, to lay out the Remainder of the Said Hundred Acres in half Acre Lotts, reserving in proper Places Sufficient Streets and a burying Place and Markett, and Such Lotts to grant and Confirm in Fee to those that will take them, upon condition that the Grantee do build thereon according to the Condition of the Said Deed.

From SR 23 pp. 100-102, 1722

An Act, for settling the Precinct Courts and Courthouses.

I. Whereas through the great Taxes and Charges this Government hath laboured under, by Means of the late Indian War, there has been no Care taken by preceding Assemblies to settle the several Precinct Courts to any fixed or Certain Place, but have always hitherto been kept and held at priivate Houses, where they have been, and are liable to be removed, at the Pleasure of the person or persons owning such Houses, to the great Annoyance of the

Magistrates and People: For the Prevention of which for the Future;

II. Be It Enacted, by his Excellency the Pallatine, and the rest of the true and absolute Lords Proprietors of the Province of Carolina, by and with the Advice and Consent of the rest of the Members of this present General Assembly, now met at Edenton, at Queen Anne's Creek, in Chowan Precinct for the North East part of the said Province, and it is hereby Enacted, by the Authority of the same, That from and after the Ratification of this Act, the Justices of the Peace that are now appointed for and in every respective Precinct in this Government, or shall hereafter be appointed within the Time limited in this Act for Building the Precinct Court-houses, or the greatest part of them, are hereby required and impowered to purchase the quantity of One Acre of Land, in such Place or Places of their several Precincts, as in and by this Act is hereby nominated and appointed, for erecting the said Court-houses on.

V. And be It Further Enacted, by the Authority aforesaid, That if the Justices, or the major part of them, in their several Precincts, shall neglect or refuse to purchase the land by this Act directed for building the several Court-houses on, or to agree with workmen to build and finish the same, (which shall not be less than Twenty Four feet Long and Sixteen Feet wide), within Six months after the Ratification of this Act; that then, and in such Case, the Governor or Commander in Chief for the Time being shall, and is hereby impowered and directed to nominate and appoint such Person or Persons in each and every Precinct so neglecting or refusing; which Person so appointed, shall have the same Power and Authority to lay the said Tax, purchase such Land, and build the said Court-houses, as the said Justices might or ought to have had by this Act.

VI. And be it Further Enacted, by the Authority aforesaid, That the Lands hereafter mentioned be, by the several Justices, or the Major Part of them, in each respective Precinct, purchased, to and for the Building and erecting the several Court-houses on: That is to say: For the Precinct of Chowan, at Edenton.

SR 25 pp. 175-178, 1722

An act for Enlarging and Encouragement of the Town called Edenton, in Chowan precinct.

Whereas, Thom's Peterson, late of Chowan Precinct, Esq'r, dyed seized in his Demesen as of Fee a certain Tract of Land or plantation lying in the Fork of Queen Ann's Creek, in Chowan precinct, containing two hundred and Seventy Acres, be the same more or less adjoining to the Lands of the Town now called Edenton, which Lands on the Decease of the Said Thom's did descend unto Ann, the Daughter of the Said Thomas; And, whereas, Johanna, the Mother of the said Ann, upon her humble petition to the General Biennial Assembly held for the Year 1715, obtained an Act of Assembly intitled an Act of impowering Johanna Peterson, Widow of Thom's Peterson, late of Albemarle County, Esq'r, to make Saile of certain Lands belonging to whom the Lands do Descend, Thereby impowering the said Johanna to make Sale of the Said Lands for the Benefit and Advantage of her said Daughter, and her better Advancement, and the Said Lands remaining as yet unsold and lying very convenient to be added to Edenton for the Enlargement of the said Town; and the said Johanna referring the Valuation thereof to the Assembly,

I. Be it Enacted by his Excellency, the Palatine, and the rest of the true and absolute Lords Proprietors of the Province of Carolina, by and with the Advice and Consent of the rest of the Members of the General Assembly, now met at Edenton, at Queen Anne's Creek, in Chowan Precinct, for the North-East Part of the said Province, and it is hereby Enacted, that the Lands already laid out for the said Town called Edenton, together with the aforesaid Tract of Land, two hundred and Seventy Acres lately belonging to the Said Tho's Peterson adjoining to the said Town, be henceforward invested in Christopher Gale, Jn'o. Lovick and Edward Mosely, Esq'rs., and Nicholas Crisp, to and for the Uses aforesaid, And declared confirmed and incorporated into a Township by the name of Edenton, with all privileges hereafter expressed for ever, pursuant to which

II. It is hereby Enacted, That the places already laid out for a Church and a Court House, a burying place and a Market place be reserved for their Uses, and that the Rest of the Land formerly invested in Daniel Richardson, Esq'r, and already laid out into Lotts of half an Acre each or there abouts be disposed of by the Commiss'r afore mentioned as hereafter in this Act is directed.

III. And be it further Enacted by the Authority aforesaid, that the two hundred and Seventy Acres of Land afore mentioned and now by this Act incorporated into the Town of Edenton be forthwith laid out into proper allottments and appropriated to and for the Uses expressed, Viz't: One hundred and forty Acres most convenient to the Creek and nearest on a Square into Lotts of half an Acre, with Convenient Streets and Passages, which Lotts so laid out shall be Sold at publick Vendue or Outcry to the highest Bidder and the Money arising thereof accounted for and paid by the Treasurer hereafter mentioned to the publick treasurer of this Governm't, in order to reimburs the Publick for the first Purchase after necessary Charges are deducted; and that the Land wherever the Houses now stand, together with eight Acres next adjacent thereunto, shall be appropriated to and for the Uses and Benefit of the Gov'r, president or Commander in Chief of this province his Residence for the time being for Ever, and the Rest and Residue of the said Land shall be, continue and remain as a Common for the Use of the Inhabitants of the Town for Ever.

Provided always, that in Case the Gov'r, president or Commander in Chief for the time being shall not think fit to reside on the Land appointed for that Use, That then and at Such Times the same shall be at the Disposal of the Commiss'rs aforesaid for the Uses of the publick 'till such Time as the Govern'r, president or Commander in Chief for the time being shall dwell thereon.

IV. And be it further Enacted by the Authority aforesaid, that the Said Christopher Gale, Esq'r, shall be present Treasurer and Receiver of all Moneys arising by the Sale of the said Lotts, and on his Death or Departure out of the Governm't then the first Commiss'r shall Succeed and be Treasurer for time being, giving Security to the Justices of the precinct Court tat he will be accountable for the Moneys he shall receive according to the Directions of this Act.

V. And be it further Enacted by the Authority aforesaid, That every person whatsoever who is willing or desirous to be an Inhabitant of the said Town shall have Liberty to take up any Lotts or Lott so laid out as aforesaid and not before taken up, which Lott or Lotts the Commiss'rs afore appointed or any three of them, whereof the Treasurer to be one, are hereby required, directed and impowered to grant, convey and acknowledge to the Persons so taking up the Same and to his Heirs and Assigns for Ever in Fee Simple, to witt, if the said Lott or Lotts be part of the One hundred and forty Acres, then upon the Consideration before expressed, and if part of the Land which was formerly laid out and invested in Daniel Richardson, Esq'r, then upon the payment of thirty shilling for each Lott, Twenty shillings whereof shall be paid to the said Daniel Richardson, Esq'r, to his Heirs and Assigns, and the other Tenn Shillings shall be appropriated to the Use of the Church, to be disposed of as by the Vestry of the N. E. parish of Chowan shall from time to time be directed and appointed.

Provided always, that what person so ever shall take and purchase as in Manner before directed and shall not build or Cause to be built thereon within two Years after the Date of the said Conveyance a good, Substantial, Habitable House, not of less Demensions that twenty feet long and fifteen feet in Width, besides sheds and Leanto's, or make Such preperations for so doing as the Commiss'rs or any two of them shall judge reasonable to secure the Same, Every such Conveyance shall be and is hereby declared Void and of None Effect as if the Same had never been made, and that the Said Lott or Lotts be free and clear for any other person to take up and purchase in Manner as is before directed.

Provided further, that all Moneys arising by the Second or other the Sales of the Said Lotts shall be and it is hereby appropriated to the Use of the parish, first for the building of a Church and afterwards to such other Uses as the Church Wardens and Vestry shall think fit, Except twenty shillings of the Money arising by the Second Sale or Lapse of Such of the Lotts as belong to the Land first laid out for the said Town, which shall be paid to the Said Daniel Richardson, Esq'r, his Heirs or Assigns.

VI. And be it further Enacted by the Authority aforesaid, that the Commiss'rs aforesaid or any to of them shall have full power and Authority and they are hereby impowered and required and Commanded to remove all Nusances within the Limitts of the afores'd Town, and that no persons Inhabitants of the Said Town or holding Lotts there shall Enclose the Same or keep the Same enclosed in the said Town, under a common Stake Fence, but every Lott or Lotts so enclosed shall be either paled in or done with posts and Rails.

VII. And also, as a further Encouragement to the Settlement of the Said Town, Be it also Enacted by the Authority aforesaid, that from and after the 25th Day of March next after the Ratification of this Act the following publick Officers shall and are hereby required under the penalty of five pounds p'r Month to keep their Several and respective Offices by themselves or Sufficient Deputies within the Said Town of Edenton, viz't:

Chief Justice	Provost Marshal	Comptroler
Secretary	for the County of Albemarle	Naval Officer
Attorney Gen'll	Escheator Gen'll	Register of Deeds and
Survey'r Gen'll	Collector	Writings in Chowan
		Receiver of Powder.

which Said Fines shall be recoverable by Bill, plaint or Information in the Gen'll Court of this province, one half to the Church Wardens and Vestry of the No. East parish of Chowan, the other half to him or them that shall Sue for the Same, and that all Musters for the Company adjoining to Edenton, Election of Burgesses and all Bussiness and Affairs of the like Nature w'h properly belong to the s'd Precinct shall be taken, don and Transacted w'thin the s'd Town of Edenton, and no other place or places whatsoever. Provided allways, that the said Officers shall not be Obliged to keep their s'd offices in the said Town untill there shall be a Councill Room & Gaol built in the said Town.

VIII. And be it further Enacted by ye authority afs'd, that all Persons possess'rs or owners of Lotts in the s'd Town shall and they are hereby Obliged within two years after the ratification of this Act to take care and Clear all such Lotts so held and possessed by them from all manner of Wood, underwood, or Grubbs that are or may be offencive to the s'd Inhabitants, and shall so keep and maintain the same from time to time and at all times hereafter as often as need shall require, under the penalty of five Shillings p'r m'th, to be recovered before any Justice of the peace, one half to the Informer & the other half to the Vestry for the use of the Parish.

IX. And be it further Enacted by the Authority aforesaid, That in Case of the Death or Departure out of the Governm't of any of the afores'd Commiss'rs at any time or times and at all times hereafter the Remaining part of the Said Commiss'rs are hereby fully authorized and impowered to make Choice of some other person or persons to Succeed Such Commiss'r or Commiss'rs so dying or departing as aforesaid, which person or persons so elected and Chosen shall and they are hereby invested with as full power and Authority to all Intents and purposes whatsoever as the present Commiss'r now herein nominated and appointed, that so the full number of the Commiss'rs may always be kept up and full.

X. And as a further Encouragement to the said Town being the Metropolis of this Governm't, it is Enacted, that at the next Biennial Election for Members of Assembly the Inhabitants of the Said Town shall have Liberty to elect a Representative to Sitt in the Gen'll Assembly, and to encourage the Better Settlement of Bath Town in Bath County.

XI. It is hereby Enacted, That at the next Biennial Election of Members of Assembly the Inhabitants of the Said Town shall have Liberty to elect a Representative for the Said Town to Sitt in the Gen'll Assembly of this province, and shall have the like Liberty in all Succeeding Assemblys.

XII. And be it further Enacted by the Authority aforesaid, that the said Johanna do receive out of the publick Treasury the Sum of two hundred and fifty pounds for the Use of her said Daughter, the same being adjudged by this assembly the full Value of the said Lands, and that the Said Johanna do give good Security for appropriating the Said Moneys to the best advantage of Ann, her Daughter; Also the sum of Fifty pounds for the Value of the improvements made by the Said Johanna.

From SR 25 pp. 191-194, 1723

An act entitled an additional act relating to biennial and other assemblies and regulating elections and divers other things relating to towns.

VI. Be it therefore Enacted by the Autho'ty aforesaid, that upon Complaints made to the Commiss'rs or any two of them of any person so offending they shall issue their Warr't to two Freeholders of the Said Town to view the Offence, and upon proof made of the Fact committed to ascertain the Damages, which are to be levied by a Warr't from the Commiss'rs or any of them on the Goods of the Offender, to be paid into the Hands of the Town Treasurer for the Use of the said Town, and for the Encouragem't of Trade and Merchants to reside in the Said Town of Edenton, being the Metropolis of this Governm't.

X. And Whereas, his Excellency the palatin and the Rest of the true and absolute Lords prop'rs have out of their Great Bounty and Zeal for promotion of true Religion and piety given two hundred pounds sterling towards the Building of a Church in Such place as the Gen'll Assembly shall think proper and suitable for Benefit of the Generality of the Inhabitants, And the Gen'll Assembly having already declared Edenton to be the metropolis of the Gov'm't.

CO5/333 pp 27-27b, 1738

An Act to appropriate 2000 pounds Current Bill money to erect a sufficient Gaol, an office or sufficient Place for the safe keeping of the records of the General Court and for repairing the Courthouse at Edenton and for other purposes therein mentioned

Whereas thro' the insufficiency of the provincial goal at Edenton, not only Debtors have escaped to the Defrauding of the creditors but also Divers felons and other criminals have broke prison and escaped with impunity to the great encouragement to Persons to Commit enormous crimes and by means hereof the administration of Justice is rendered ineffectual and Whereas not only an office or place for the safekeeping the records of the General Court and for the clerk of the said Court to transact his Business and where he may give due attendence and any person may have recourse and apply to search any Record or get copies of such Records or papers as they should require but also several necessary reparations to the said courthouse at Edenton are very much wanted, wherefore we pray that it may be enacted. . . . And be it enacted by his excellency the Governor, Council, and General Assembly that the Honorable Wm. Smith Esquire, John Montgomery Esquire, Mr. John Hodgson, Mr. Joseph Andersen, Mr Thomas Luten, Mr. John Blount, and Mr. Jacob Butler be and they are hereby appointed Commissioners or Trustees for erecting and Building a Provincial Goal in Edenton on the Lott for that purpose laid out and appointed and an office or place for the safe keeping of the records of the General Court on the lott which the Courthouse is Built and to repair the said Courthouse at Edenton, which said Commissioners or the Majority of them are hereby impowered to erect and build the said Gaol and office of Brick but in the dimensions and in such manner as they shall think proper and to make such repairs on to the said Courthouse as they shall think necessary so that the charge of the building, the said Gaol and office and repairing the said Courthouse do not exceed 2000 pounds by this Act appropriate for this Purpose. And be it enacted by the authority aforesaid that for defraying the charge of Building this Gaol and repairing the said courthouse and building the office aforesaid, the sheriff of each county is hereby Impowered and Authorized at any time before the first day of July next after the ratification of this Act and also at any time before the first day of July in the next succeeding year and not longer Demand, levy upon and receive from the inhabitants of this province the sum of 2s current bills as a Poll tax for every tithable person of the counties of the Province and in case of the refusal of payment to be recovered by the said sheriff in the same Manner by Distress as is directed in the Act of Assembly for collecting and recovering all Publick Levies already established.
Wm. Downing, Speaker
Wm. Smith
Gabriel Johnston

From SR 23 pp. 136-141, 1740

An Act, for Confirming Titles to the Town Lands of Edenton, for securing the Priviledges heretofore granted to the said Town, and for further Encouragement and better Regulation thereof.

I. Whereas, Pursuant to the several Acts of Assembly of this Province heretofore passed and Ratified, Four Hundred and Twenty Acres of Land, lying in the Fork of Queen Ann's Creek, in Chowan County, in the Province aforesaid, bounded Eastward, by the Lands of Miles Gales; Northward, by the Lands of William Badham, deceased, and George Lisles; on the Westward, by the Beaver Dam and Creek, and on the Southward, by the Sound, was purchased by the Public, and hath been laid out for a Town, called Edenton, and part thereof divided into Lots of Half Acres, as will more fully appear by the Plan thereof, already laid out, with convenient Streets, Passages, Place for a Church, Governour's House, Court House, Burying Place, Market Place, and Council Room and other Purposes And, by the said Act, were vested, in Fee, in Commissioners or Trustees, to dispose thereof according to the Directions of the said several Acts, many of which Commissioners or Trustees have conveyed Lots or Half Acres to several Persons, who built thereon, and have made a considerable improvement; and the Residue of the said Four Hundred and Twenty Acres was reserved for a Town Common.

II. And whereas several of the said Acts have been since repealed, expired, or stand suspended, whereby many Inconveniencies and Mischiefs, may arise, the Improvement and building of the said Town very much retarded, the Power of the Commissioners and Trustees become dubious, and the Persons Titles to such Lots Precarious: For Remedy whereof, and to Prevent Disputes that may happen, and for the better securing the ancient Priviledges of the said Township, and Regulation thereof.

III. We pray that it may be Enacted, And be it Enacted, by his Excellency Gabriel Johnston, Esq., Governor, by and with the Advice and Consent of his Majesty's Council, and General Assembly of this Province, and by the Authority of the same, That the said Four Hundred and Twenty Acres, so purchased and laid out for the said Town of Edenton, pursuant to the said Acts of Assembly, and vested in Commissioners or Trustees, according to the said several Acts, such Commissioners or Trustees so invested, are hereby declared to have a good absolute, and indefeasible Estate, in fee, in such Lands respectively, in Trust and Confidence, to and for the uses of the said several Acts, and the Commissioners and Trustees hereafter mentioned, are hereby declared to have a good, absolute, and indefeasible Estate, in Fee, in all such Lands and Lots which have not been disposed of by the former Commissioners or Trustees, but in Trust and Confidence, to and for the Use and Uses hereinafter mentioned relating to the said Town of Edenton, and for no other Use or Purpose whatsoever; and the said Lands and Lots are hereby Confirmed to the said Commissioners or Trustees in Fee, to such Use or Uses, Anything in the Repealing, Expiring, Suspension of any of the said Acts, or any other Law, Statute, Usage, or Custom, to the Contrary, notwithstanding.

IV. And be it further Enacted by the Authority aforesaid, That if any Person or Persons have Purchased and paid for any Lot or Lots, Half Acre or Half Acres of Land in said Town of Edenton, of any of the Commissioners or Trustees, pursuant to the said several Acts, and have fully complied with the Conditions in the said several Acts mentioned, such Person or Persons are hereby declared to be vested with, and to have a Good, absolute, and indefeasible Estate, in Fee, to such Lot or Lots, Half Acre or Half Acres of Land; and the same is hereby confirmed, in fee, to such Person or Persons, and to his, her, and their Heirs and Assigns, forever.

V. And be it further Enacted, by the Authority aforesaid, That the Honourable William Smith, Esq.; John Hodgson, Esq.; Abraham Blackball, Joseph Anderson, and James Craven, Gentlemen, are hereby appointed Commissioners or Trustees, to and for the several Uses and Purposes declared by this Act, and Impowered and invested with all the Priviledges hereafter expressed, forever.

VIII. And be it further Enacted, by the Authority aforesaid, That the Lots of Half an Acre each, or thereabouts, not taken up and disposed of, be disposed of by the Commissioners or Trustees aforesaid, as hereafter in this Act is directed.

IX. And be it further Enacted, by the Authority aforesaid, That the Places already laid out, as by the Plan of the said Town may more fully appear, for Streets, Passages, Church, Governour's House, Court House, Burying Place, Market Place, Prison, Council Room, and Town Common, be reserved for those Uses, and no other.

XI. Provided always, That if any Person or Persons whatsoever, shall take up and purchase any Lot or Lots, as in Manner before directed, and shall not build, or cause to be built thereon, for each and every Lot or Lots so taken up and purchased, within Two Years after the Date of the said Conveyance, a good, substantial, Brick, Stone, or framed Habitable House, not of less Dimensions than Twenty Feet long, Fifteen Feet in Width, and Eight Feet in Height, between the first floor and the Joists, or in Proportion for each and every Lot or Lots, or make such Preparation for so doing as the Commissioners, or the Majority of them, shall judge reasonable to secure the same, every such Conveyance shall be, and is hereby declared void and of none effect, as if the same had never been made; and that the same Lots be free and clear for any other Person to take up and purchase, as in Manner before directed.

XIII. And be it further Enacted, by the Authority aforesaid, That if any Person, after the First Day of May next, shall erect, repair, or cause to be erected or repaired any Wooden Chimney within the said Town, such Person so offending, shall forfeit and pay, for each and every offence, the Sum of Ten Pounds Proclamation Money; to be recovered and appropriated as hereafter by this Act is directed.

XIV. And be it further Enacted, by the Authority aforesaid, That the Commissioners or Trustees as aforesaid, or any Three of them, shall within Six Months after the Ratification of this Act, meet and lay a Tax on each and every Person, according to the Number of his or her Lot or Lots, Half Acre or Half Acres of Land, by him or them held within the said Town (Fronts excepted), sufficient to raise a Fence round the said Town, and Town Common, as the Commissioners or Trustees aforesaid, or any Three of them, shall think sufficient, so as the said Fence be compleated within Eighteen Months after the Ratification of this Act; under the Penalty of Five Pounds Proclamation Money, on each and every Commissioner: And in

Case any Person or Persons shall neglect or refuse to pay, on Demand, his or her Tax so laid by the aforesaid Commissioners or Trustees, by Virtue of this Act, such Person or Persons so Offending, shall forfeit and pay the Sum of Two Shillings and Six Pence Proclamation Money, over and above the said Tax, for each and every Lot he or she hath a Conveyance for; to be recovered and appropriated as hereafter in this Act is directed.

XV. And be it further Enacted, by the Authority aforesaid, That if any evil minded Person shall, in the Night, or at any Time or Times, whatsoever, pull down the said Town Fence, or any Part thereof, in Order to let in any Person's Hogs, Cattle, or Horses, within the said Town Inclosure, or shall otherwise drive pigs, Cattle or Horses, into or out of the said Town, such Person so offending shall forfeit and pay, for each and every Offence, the Sum of Ten Pounds Proclamation Money; to be recovered and appropriated as by this Act is hereafter directed.

XXI. And be it further Enacted, by the Authority aforesaid, That the Right and Privilege of Electing a Representative for the said Town of Edenton, to sit in the General Assembly be, and is hereby confirmed, that the Freeholders of the said Town shall, forever, have liberty, at all Times hereafter, to elect and choose a Member to sit in General Assembly; and a Writ of Election shall issue, to the Inhabitants of the said Town, to choose a Member to represent them in the said Assembly, at such Times, and in the same Manner, as the said Writs are issued for choosing Representatives for the several Counties in this Province to sit in the General Assembly.

XXIV. And be it further Enacted, by the Authority aforesaid, That the Treasurer of the said Town, from and after the Ratification of this Act, shall be obliged to keep his Office, and a Plan of the Town, in the said Town, under the Penalty of One Pound Proclamation Money, for each and every month he shall neglect or refuse to do the same to be recovered and appropriated as by this Act is hereafter directed.

XXVII. And be it further Enacted, by the Authority aforesaid, That an Act, passed in the Year One Thousand Seven Hundred and Thirty Eight, intituled an Act for Encouragement and better Regulation of the Town of Edenton, and every Clause, Matter, and thing therein contained, shall be, and is hereby Repealed and made null and void, to all Intents and Purposes whatsoever.

SR 23 p. 181, 1741

An Act, for the building and maintaining Court-houses, Prisons and Stocks, in every County within this Province, and appointing Rules to each County Prison for Debtors.

I. We pray that it may be Enacted, And be it Enacted by his Excellency Gabriel Johnston, Esq., Governor, By and with the Advice and Consent of his Majesty's Council, and General Assembly of this Province, and is hereby Enacted, by the Authority of the same, That the Justices in all and every County or Counties within this Province, where there is not already suitable provision made, shall, and are hereby impowered and required, at the next succeeding Court of their respective Counties, after the Ratification of this Act, to lay a sufficient Levy upon the Inhabitants of the said Counties, not exceeding One Shilling, Proclamation Money per Poll, for Two Years, for the building a Court House, Prison and Stocks, or any such of them as shall be wanting; which Levy shall be paid and collected by the Sheriff of each County, in the same Manner as all other Public and Parish Taxes and levies are paid and collected, and by him shall be accounted for to the Justices of the County Court, upon Oath; and the said Sheriff shall be allowed Three per Cent. for Collecting the same.

II. And be it further Enacted, by the Authority aforesaid, That the Justices of each County shall and may, from Time to Time, and at all Times hereafter, employ Persons to keep and maintain the Court-House, Prison and Stocks, already Built, and such as are to be built, by Virtue of this or any other Act, or to rebuild such as have fallen to Decay and Ruin, and the same be kept in good Repair, by laying a Poll Tax on the Inhabitants of their respective Counties as aforesaid.

III. And be it further Enacted, by the Authority aforesaid, That if any Person shall neglect or refuse to pay the aforesaid Levies, in Manner aforesaid, and shall be in Arrear after the last Day of Payment, such Person shall be liable to double Distress; to be levied on his Goods and Chattels by the Sheriff of the County where such Delinquent inhabits And for the Preservation of the Health of such Persons as shall, at any Time hereafter, be committed to the County Prisons, the Court shall have Power to Mark out such Parcel of Land as they shall think fit, not exceeding Six Acres, adjoining to the Prison, for the Rules thereof; and every Prisoner, not committed for Treason or Felony, giving good Security to the Sheriff of the County to keep within the said Rules, shall have Liberty to walk therein out of the Prison, for the Preservation of his or their Health: And every Prisoner giving such Security as aforesaid, and keeping continually within the said Rules, shall be, and is hereby adjudged and declared to be, in Law a true Prisoner; and that every Person therewith concerned may know the true Bounds of the said Rules, the same shall be recorded in the County Records, and the Marks thereof shall, from Time to Time, be renewed, as Occasion shall require.

SR 25 p. 341, 1756

An Act for Laying a Tax for repairing the Court House in Edenton.

I. Whereas, the Court House in Edenton whereat the Supreme Court for the Countys of Currituck, Pasquotank, Perquimons, Chowan, Bertie and Tyrril, is by Law Directed to be held, is in a ruinous Condition and great Decay; wherefore, that the same may be Decently repaired.

II. Be it Enacted, by the Governor, Council and Assembly, and by the Authority of the same, That a poll Tax of Eight pence per Taxable be laid on each Taxable person in the County of Chowan for two years next Ensuing, which Tax shall be Collected by the Sheriff of the said County, in the same manner and at such time as Publick Taxes are by Law Directed to be Collected, and by him Accounted for and paid to the Commissioners appointed for erecting an Office and Prison at Edenton, aforesaid; And shall be by them applied to the repairing the said Court House in a neat, Decent and Workmanlike manner.

III. And whereas, a Tax has been laid on the Countys of Currituck, Pasquotank, Perquimons, Chowan, Bertie and Tyrril, for Erecting an office and Prison in Edenton.

IV. Be it Enacted, by the Authority aforesaid, That if any Surplus shall remain after the said Office and Prison shall be Built, such Surplus shall be, with the Tax hereby laid, applied towards repairing the said Court House.

V. And be it further Enacted, by the Authority aforesaid, That the Commissioners aforesaid shall, with all Convenient speed, Cause the said Court House to be repaired as aforesaid, and on Oath, thereafter render an account of the Monies by them received by Virtue of this Act, together with that of their Disbursements, to the County Court of Chowan.

From SR 23 pp. 483-484, 1758

An Act to enable the Commissioners of Port Roanoke, to amend the Navigation of the said Port; and for other Purposes.

I. Whereas, from the bad Condition of the Channel from Beacon Island, through the Swatch, the Trade and Commerce of the Northern Parts of this province is greatly prejudiced; and it having been represented to this Assembly by the Commissioners of Port Roanoke, that by removing certain Shoals, a better Channel may be made to Roanoke Bar, and that they have employed a skillful Person to undertake the same; Wherefore to enable the said Commissioners to accomplish the said Undertaking, in the most effectual Manner.

II. Be it Enacted, by the Governor, Council and Assembly, and by the Authority of the same, That from and after the passing of this Act, instead of the Powder and Lead Duty payable in the said Port of Roanoke, the Receiver of the said Duty, for and during the Space of Five Years, shall receive the same in Proclamation Money at the Rate of Two Shillings per Ton, for every Vessel that shall enter in the said Port; the Tonnage of which Vessel shall be ascertained agreeable to the Directions of an Act of Assembly, intituled, An Act to amend and continue An Act intituled, An Act for granting to his Majesty a Duty upon the Tonnage of Ships and other Vessels coming into this Province, for the Purposes therein mentioned; which Duty the said Receiver shall, from Time to Time, after deducting Five per Centum, and no more for his Commissions, pay to the Order of the Commissioners of the said Port, to be employed and laid out in mending the Channel, and improving of the same, in such Manner as they shall think most beneficial and serviceable for the Public.

SR 23 pp. 683-684, 1766

An Act for erecting a Court House and Prison, for the use of the District of Edenton.

I. Whereas it is necessary that a new Court House and Prison should be built for the Use of the District of Edenton;

II. Be it therefore Enacted, by the Governor, Council, and Assembly, and by the Authority of the same, That Mr. Cullen Pollock, Mr. Joseph Hewes, Mr. Thomas Nash, Mr. Edward Vail, and Mr. William Lowther, be, and are hereby nominated and appointed Trustees and

Directors, for building and erecting a good and convenient Court House, and sufficient Prison, for the Use of the District aforesaid; and for that Purpose, to contract and agree with proper Persons for compleating and Finishing the said Court House and Prison, in such Manner as they shall think necessary and Convenient.

III. And be it further Enacted, by the Authority aforesaid, That a Poll Tax of One Shilling be levied on each Taxable Person within the County of Chowan, and of Four Pence on each taxable Person within the Counties of Currituck, Pasquotank, Perquimons, Bertie, Tyrrel, and Hertford; to be collected for the present and next succeeding Years, by the Sheriffs of the said Counties respectively, and accounted for and paid to the said Trustees and Directors, at the same time, in the same manner, and under the like Penalties as is by Law directed for collecting, accounting for, and paying Public taxes.

IV. And whereas by an Act of Assembly passed at New Bern, in the Year of our Lord One Thousand Seven Hundred and Fifty Eight, for applying certain Monies, to be collected on the Tonnage of Vessels, to enable the Commissioners of Port Roanoke to amend the Navigation of the said Port, and for other Purposes; and whereas the said Monies never have Been, or is there any Probability that the same ever will be applied for the Purposes aforesaid, but still remain in the Hands of the Commissioners, or the Receiver of the said Duty: Be it therefore Enacted by the Authority aforesaid, That the said Commissioners, and the said Receiver, shall, immediately from and after the passing of this Act, pay to the Trustees and Directors, for building the said Court House and Prison, all such Sum and Sums of Money as shall remain in their Hands not applied agreeable to the Act of Assembly aforesaid; and to be replaced and refunded at such Time, and in such Manner, as the Governor, Council, and Assembly, shall think Proper.

V. And be it further Enacted, by the Authority aforesaid, That from and after the passing of this Act, the said Trustees and Directors are hereby required and impowered to sell and dispose of, for the best Price that may be had, the old Court House, Prison, and other Public Buildings, that are now standing on the Public Lots in the Town of Edenton.

VI. And be it further Enacted, by the Authority aforesaid, That the said Trustees and Directors shall apply all such Monies as shall come to their Hands in Virtue of this Act, and such other Sum or Sums of Money as they shall obtain by the Voluntary Donations of Gentlemen and others, towards building and erecting the said Court House and Prison, in such Manner as to the said Trustees and Directors shall seem most convenient.

VII. And be it further Enacted, by the Authority aforesaid, That before the said Trustees and Directors shall enter upon their said Trust, or take into their Hands any of the Monies aforesaid, they shall enter into Bond, in the Sum of Two Thousand Pounds, payable to his Excellency the Governor, and to his Successors, with Condition for the faithful Discharge of the several Trusts in them reposed by this Act; and that they will, from Time to Time, and at all Times when they shall be called upon, lay a Just State of their Transactions before the Assembly, or such Committee as shall be appointed to settle and adjust the Public Accounts; which Bond shall be lodged with the Clerk of the Superior Court for the District of Edenton.

VIII. And be it Enacted, by the Authority aforesaid, That if the Taxes, or other Monies arising in Virtue of this Act, shall be more than sufficient to compleat the Buildings herein directed, the Surplus thereof shall, by the Trustees herein Named, be paid to the Court of Each County, in Proportion to the Number of Taxables collected from each of the said Counties, and paid by the Sheriff to the Trustees.

SR 23 pp. 929-930, 1773

An Additional Act to an Act for erecting a Court House and Prison Use of the District of Edenton.

I. Whereas the several Funds appropriated by the before recited Act, have been found inadequate to the Purposes thereby intended.

II. Be it therefore Enacted, by the Governor, Council, and Assembly, and by the Authority of the same, That a Poll Tax of Two Shillings be levied on each Taxable Person within the County of Chowan, and of Eight Pence on each taxable Person within the Counties of Currituck, Pasquotank, Perquimans, Bertie, Tyrrell, and Hertford, to be collected for this and the Two next succeeding Years, by the Sheriff of the said Counties respectively, and accounted for and paid to the Trustees and Directors mentioned in the before recited Act, or to the Survivors of them, at the same Time, in the same Manner; and under the like Penalties, as by Law is directed for collecting, accounting for and paying Public Taxes.

III. And be it further Enacted, by the Authority aforesaid, That the said Trustees and Directors shall apply all such Monies as shall come to their Hands in Virtue of this Act, to the Purposes directed in the before recited Act; and shall enter into Bond, in the sum of Two Thousand Pounds, Payable to his Excellency the Governor, and to his Successors, with Condition for the faithful Discharge, of the Trust in them reposed by this Act; and that they will from Time to Time, and at all times when they shall be called upon, lay a just State of their Transactions before the Assembly, or such Committee as shall be appointed to settle and adjust the Public Accounts; which Bond shall be lodged with the Clerk of the Superior Court for the District of Edenton.

IV. And be it further Enacted, by the Authority aforesaid, That if the Tax arising in Virtue of this Act should be more than Sufficient to compleat the Buildings as mentioned in the before recited Act, the Surplus thereof shall by the Trustees and Directors be paid to the Court of each County, in Proportion to the Sum collected from each of the said Counties, and paid by the Sheriff to the said Trustees and Directors.

V. And be it further Enacted, by the Authority aforesaid, That the said Gaol when finished, shall be deemed the proper Prison for the Commitment and Confinement of all Traitors, Felons, and other notorious Criminals, who shall be apprehended in any of the Counties constituting the said District; and the Sheriff, Coroner, or other Officer, who shall have such Criminal in Custody, shall have full Power and Authority to convey him to the said Gaol and deliver him to the Sheriff of Chowan County, or to the Keeper of the said Gaol, with the Mittimus, or Paper containing the Cause of such Commitment; which Sheriff or Keeper of the said Gaol, is hereby commanded and required to receive into the said Gaol, all such Prisoners delivered to him as aforesaid, and shall give to such Sheriff, Coroner, or other Officer, from whom he shall receive such Prisoner, a Receipt, acknowledging that he has received into his Custody such Prisoner and Mittimus, or Paper containing and setting forth the Cause of the Commitment; and shall retain all Persons committed in Virtue of this Act in close Gaol, until they shall be released by due Course of Law.

Read three times, and ratified in open Assembly, the sixth Day of March, A. D., 1773.

JOSIAH MARTIN, ESQUIRE, Governor.
James Hasell, President.
JOHN HARVEY, Speaker.

SR 24 pp. 144-145, 1777

An Act for erecting a Prison in the Town of Edenton, for the Use of the District of Edenton.

I. Whereas it is necessary that a new Prison should be built for the Use of the District of Edenton;

II. Be it therefore Enacted by the General Assembly of the State of North Carolina, and it is hereby Enacted by the Authority of the same, That Joseph Hewes, William Bennett, and Charles Bonfield, Esqrs., be, and they are hereby nominated and appointed Trustees and Directors for building and erecting a good and sufficient Prison for the Use of the District aforesaid, and for that Purpose to contract and agree with proper Persons for compleating and finishing the said Prison, in such Manner as they shall think necessary and convenient.

III. And be it further Enacted, by the Authority aforesaid, That an Assessment of one Shilling be levied on each Hundred Pounds Value within the County of Chowan, and of Six Pence on each Hundred Pounds Value within the Counties of Currituck, Pasquotank, Perquimans, Bertie, Tyrrell, Hertford, and Cambden, for Two Years, to be collected for the present and succeeding Year by the Sheriffs or Collectors of the said Counties respectively, and accounted for and paid to the said Trustees and Directors, at the same Time, in the same Manner, and under the like Penalties and Restrictions, as by Law is directed for collecting, accounting for, and paying Public Taxes.

IV. And be it further Enacted, by the Authority aforesaid, That before the said Trustees and Directors shall enter upon their said Trust, or take into their Hands any of the Monies aforesaid, they shall enter into Bond, in the sum of Three Thousand Pounds, payable to the Justices of the County Court of Chowan, and their Successors, with Condition for the faithful Discharge of the Trusts in them reposed by this Act.

V. And be it further Enacted, by the Authority aforesaid, That if the Taxes arising by Virtue of this Act shall be more than sufficient to compleat the Buildings herein directed, the Surplus thereof shall by the Trustees herein named be paid to the Court of each County, in Proportion to the Taxes collected from each of the said Counties, and paid by the Sheriffs to the Trustees.

From SR 24 pp. 238-240, 1778

An Act to amend an Act, intitled an Act for Erecting a Prison in the Town of Edenton for the use of the District of Edenton, and other Purposes.

I. Whereas, the provision heretofore made for Erecting a Prison for the District of Edenton from the Great Scarcity & High Prices of Materials and the Difficulty of obtaining workmen is now insufficient to answer the purposes thereby intended; and, whereas, the Court House of the Said District is in want of some repairs which may now be done at a Small Expence but if Neglected will require a Considerable Sum for that purpose.

II. Be it therefore Enacted by the General Assembly and it is hereby Enacted by the authority of the same, That Joseph Hews, William Bennett, Charles Bonafield and Josiah Collins, Esquires, be and they are hereby nominated and appointed, Trustees and Directors for building and Erecting a Good and Sufficient Prison for the use of the District aforesaid, and for that purpose to Contract and agree with proper persons for Compleating and finishing the said Prison, in such Manner as they shall think Necessary and Convenient, and for making such repairs to the Court House of the said District as may be Necessary.

III. And be it further enacted by the Authority aforesaid, That an Assessment of One Shilling be levied on each Hundred pounds value within the County of Chowan, and of six pence on each Hundred pounds value within the County of Currituck, Pasquotank, Perquimans, Bertie, Tyrrel, Hertford, Camden and Gates for Two years to be collected for, the present and succeeding year by the Sheriffs or Collectors of the said Counties respectively exclusive of the Tax laid by the said before recited Act and shall be accounted for and paid to the said Trustees and directors at the same time in the same manner and under the like penalties and restrictions as by law is directed for collecting, accounting for and paying Public Taxes and shall be by the said Trustees & Directors applyed to the purposes of this Act, and the before recited Act, and also to the payment of such Ballance as may appear on Settlement to be due to the Trustees and directors heretofore appointed for erecting a Court House and Prison for the use of the District of Edenton.

IV. And whereas, in some of the Counties in said District no assessment was made, or Tax collected in the year 1778 for the purposes intended by the before recited Act, be it therefore Enacted by the Authority aforesaid, that the Sheriffs & Collectors of such counties as have neglected to pay the said Tax in the year 1778 shall and are hereby authorized and impowered to collect such arrears of Taxes at the time of their next Collection to the intent and purpose that the whole of the said Tax laid by the before recited Act, and by this Act may be duly Collected and paid in for the purposes aforesaid.

V. And whereas, no provision hath been made for the purchase of one or more Lotts in the Town of Edenton, whereupon the said Prison may be erected.

VI. Be it therefore Enacted by the authority aforesaid, That the said Trustees and Directors, or a majority of them be, and they are hereby impowered to purchase one or more Lotts in the said Town for the purpose aforesaid and to take one or more Deeds to themselves in trust for the use, benefit and behoof of the State of North Carolina in fee simple and that such lotts be hereafter improved for the purposes aforesaid.

VII. And whereas, it is highly necessary that the said prison be erected as soon as possible and there may be occasion for money for carrying on and compleating the said prison and Court House before the said Tax can be Collected.

VIII. Be it therefore Enacted by the authority aforesaid, That the said Trustees and Directors be and they are hereby impowered to Borrow as much money as they shall think necessary not exceeding the sum of three thousand pounds to bear interest at the rate of six per cent. per annum to be paid as soon as sufficient of the said Tax shall be received for that purpose.

IX. And be it further enacted by the authority aforesaid, That before the said Trustees and Directors shall enter upon their said Trust, or to take into their hands any of the moneys aforesaid they shall enter into bond in the sum of Five thousand pounds payable to the Justices of the County Court of Chowan and their successors with condition for the faithful Discharge of the trusts in them reposed by this Act and the before recited Act.

X. And be it further enacted by the authority aforesaid, That if the Taxes arising by virtue of this Act and the before recited Act, shall be more than sufficient to compleat the purposes herein directed the surplus thereof, shall by the trustees herein named be paid to the Court of each county in proportion to the Taxes collected from each of he said Counties and paid by the Sheriffs to the said Trustees & Directors.

SR 24 pp. 452-454, 1782

An Act for regulating the town of Edenton.

I. Whereas it is the interest of every State to regulate the police of its seaport towns, and encourage their trade, and whereas the laws hitherto passed for regulating the town of Edenton have proved very defective, and the method in use of appointing commissioners for the town is inconsistent with the spirit of our present constitution;

II. Be it therefore enacted by the General Assembly of the State of North Carolina, and it is hereby enacted by the authority of the same, That five commissioners for the town of Edenton shall be chosen annually on the first Monday in July of every year, in the presence of the sheriff, or any two justices of the peace, for the county of Chowan, and every freeholder who is resident in the said town, and every free man who has resided there for twelve months, and paid public taxes, shall be qualified to vote for such commissioners, which commissioners when chosen, shall have all the powers, and be possessed of all the rights and authorities, in respect to titles to public lots, or otherwise, which any former commissioners had, and were possessed of, so far as is consistent with the perview of this Act, any former act, custom or law to the contrary notwithstanding.

III. And be it further enacted by the authority aforesaid, That the said commissioners may surround the town with a ditch or fence, erecting proper gates on the highways, they shall keep the public streets and bridges in good repair, they shall cause a public market house to be erected in some convenient place in the town, and a public wharf to be erected opposite to some street or public lot.

IV. And be it further enacted by the authority aforesaid, That the said commissioners may let out public lots on the bay that are not immediately wanted for public use, or buildings, on lease for any term not exceeding fifteen years, the rents to be applied to the use of the town.

V. And be it further enacted by the authority aforesaid, That the said commissioners shall enjoy and exercise all the powers that have been granted to former commissioners respecting the laying out of streets, and regulating of buildings, and in case they find that any building encroaches on the street they shall either cause the same to be withdrawn, or compromise with the owner for a certain annual rent to be paid for the use of the town.

VI. And be it further enacted by the authority aforesaid, That every person who is the owner of any lot in the town of Edenton, shall within six months after the passing of this act, cause the same to be cleared from woods and brush, and he shall keep it clear; that no inhabitant of the town, or other person, shall be permitted to keep hogs, goats or other stock, to graze at large in the commons, except horses and black cattle, and the number of these that may be kept by every free man inhabitant of the town, shall be regulated by the commissioners; no person shall strain a horse in any public street in the town so as to endanger the life of children, or other helpless inhabitants: every person offending contrary to these regulations, or any other laws for regulating the police of the town of Edenton, shall be fined by the trustees in any sum not exceeding twenty shillings, to be recovered before any justice of the peace, for the use of the town, and they may appoint a clerk, who shall keep a fair and compleat record of their proceedings, and be allowed for the same out of any public monies in the hands of the treasurer of said town, such sum as the commissioners shall deem adequate to his services.

VII. And be it further enacted, by the authority aforesaid, That the commissioners for the town of Edenton for the time being, shall be, and in all things act, as a body corporate, that they may plead or be impleaded as such, and bring any action against any person whatsoever for any injury done to any public building or lots in the said town, in the same manner as any private person might do for any injury done to any private property, and the intervention of the annual election shall not be considered to dissolve the body corporate, so as to abate any action depending in any court wherein the said body corporate is a party, but the new commissioners shall in every respect, and to all intents and purposes, (except as to any responsibility for any abuse of office) be considered on the same footing, and standing in the place of their predecessors, and a majority of the commissioners shall be held sufficient to decide upon any business. Provided, That no meeting of the commissioners be held to decide upon any public business, unless notice of the intended meeting, signed by one of the commissioners, shall have been left at the dwelling house of each commissioner, at least twenty four hours before the said meeting.

VIII. And be it further enacted by the authority aforesaid, That the said commissioners may levy on every lot in the town of Edenton, a tax not exceeding ten shillings specie per annum and they may lay a tax not exceeding ten shillings specie per annum, on every free man who has been resident in the said town for six months; and in case any person thus taxed shall refuse to pay the same during thirty days after notice of the same in writing, he shall be liable to an action of debt, to be brought by the said commissioners in any court of record, and if judgment shall go against him, the court may assess a fine on the said defendant not exceeding one half of the debt so recovered, over and above the said debt, to be also applied to the use of the town.

IX. And whereas the courthouse in Edenton has been much injured, and is subject to repeated injuries, from the want of proper care; Be it therefore enacted by the authority aforesaid, That the commissioners aforesaid shall repair the said court house and keep it in order, for which repairs they shall be paid out of such money as has been collected, or may hereafter be collected, for the purpose of erecting a prison house in the town of Edenton, for the District of Edenton.

X. And be it further enacted by the authority aforesaid, That the commissioners shall appoint one of their body to act as a treasurer, to receive and account for all public monies, of which a regular entry must be made in a book to be kept for that purpose, and upon the appointment of a new treasurer the old one shall immediately pass his accounts with him, and pay any balance remaining in his hands. Provided, That before such treasurer enters upon his office, he shall give bond with good security, payable to the commissioners, and conditioned for the faithful discharge of his duty.

XI. And be it further enacted by the authority aforesaid, That each commissioner, before he enters on his office, shall take, and he is required in the presence of two justices of the peace, to take the following oath: I, A. B. do swear, that I will faithfully discharge the office and duty of a commissioner for the town of Edenton, agreeable to law, according to the best of my judgment. So help me God.

XII. And be it further enacted by the authority aforesaid, That all and every former Act or Acts passed for the regulation of the town of Edenton, so far as the same, or any part thereof, is or are inconsistent with this Act, is and are hereby repealed and made void.

SR 24 pp. 455-456, 1782

An Act for building a Prison in the Town of Edenton.

I. Whereas it is represented that from the want of a prison in the town of Edenton, for the District of Edenton, the civil administration of justice is nearly at a stand, and the military service of the State greatly retarded;

II. Be it therefore enacted by the General Assembly of the State of North Carolina, and it is hereby enacted by the authority of the same, That Josiah, Collins, Michael Payne, Joseph Blount, Nathaniel Allen and Joseph Smith, be, and they are hereby appointed commissioners for building a good and sufficient prison for the use of the District of Edenton, in the town of Edenton, and for the purpose of contracting and agreeing with proper persons to compleat and finish the same, in such manner as they shall think sufficient.

III. And be it further enacted by the authority aforesaid, That an assessment of eight pence in every hundred pounds be laid on all taxable property in the county of Chowan, and an assessment of four pence in every hundred pounds value be laid on all taxable property in the Counties of Currituck, Cambden, Pasquotank, Perquimons, Gates, Hertford, Bertie and Tyrrell, for two years, to be collected for the present and the succeeding year by the respective sheriffs or collectors of the said counties, and accounted for and paid to the said commissioners at the same time, and in the same manner, and under the like penalties and restrictions, as is or may be directed for collecting, accounting for, and paying other public taxes.

IV. And be it further enacted by the authority aforesaid, That before the said commissioners shall enter upon their trust, or take into their hands any of the monies to be collected by this Act, they shall enter into bond in the sum of two thousand Spanish milled dollars, payable to the Governor and commander in chief for the time being of this State, and his successors conditioned for the faithful discharge of the trust reposed in them.

V. And whereas by an Act of the General Assembly of this State in the second year of our independence, intituled, An Act for erecting a prison in the town of Edenton, for the use of the District of Edenton, a tax was laid for raising money towards building a prison in the town aforesaid, and as it is alleged that the sheriff or collectors in the several counties in the district aforesaid have refused or neglected to pay the greatest part of the monies by them collected, into the hands of the trustees and directors mentioned in the aforesaid Act, under pretence of its small value from the great progress of depreciation; Be it therefore enacted by the authority aforesaid, that every person who have collected or received any monies in consequence of the Act recited, and for the purposes therein mentioned, shall pay, and they are hereby required to pay to the commissioners herein mentioned, the several sums by them received, with depreciation from the time it was their duty to have paid or accounted for the same; and on their refusal thus to pay, the commissioners aforesaid shall proceed against them by an action on the case, which monies thus received or recovered shall be applied to the uses mentioned in this law.

VI. And be it further enacted by the authority aforesaid, That if the different sums that may be collected in consequence of the assessments directed to be made, or referred to in this Act, shall be more than sufficient for building a prison, the balance shall be paid to the chairman of the county court of Chowan, for the time being, who shall cause it to be applied towards repairing the court house in the town of Edenton, or to be returned to the county courts of the several counties in which it was collected, and in such proportions as it was paid by those counties respectively.

SR 24 p. 594, 1784

An Act to impower the several County Courts therein mentioned to lay a Tax annually for the purpose of erecting or repairing the Court House, Prison and Stocks in each County where necessary, and for defraying the contingent charges of the County.

I. Be it Enacted by the General Assembly of the State of North Carolina, and it is hereby Enacted by the authority of the same, That the county court of each county herein mentioned viz. Chowan, Halifax, Cambden, Edgecomb, Caswell, Wake, Washington, Onslow, Northampton, Currituck, Montgomery, Pasquotank, Hertford, Bertie, Tyrrell, Cumberland, Anson, Nash, Richmond, Brunswick, Orange, Craven, Bladen, Jones, Carteret, Chatham, Burke and Dobbs shall and the same are hereby authorised and impowered from and after the passing of this Act to lay a tax annually not exceeding the sum of four shillings current money on every hundred pounds of taxable property in their county, and a poll-tax of four shillings current money on every taxable person in the said county, for the purpose of erecting, finishing or repairing such court house, prison or stocks, in any county within this State, when the same may be found by the said court to be absolutely necessary, and for the purpose of defraying the contingent charges; which said tax shall be collected and accounted for in the same manner, at the same time and by the same persons who are appointed to collect the public tax in each county, and to be paid into the hands of such person or persons as the several county courts shall from time to time hereafter direct: Provided, That a majority of the acting justices of any court wherein any tax shall be laid in virtue hereof shall be present at the time of laying the same.

II. And be it further Enacted by the authority aforesaid, That all and every Act and Acts so far as they come within the purview of this Act be, and they are hereby repealed and made void.

SR 24 pp. 873-874, 1786

An Act for Levying a Tax in the District of Edenton, for Building the Gaol of the Said District.

Whereas the tax levied for the purpose of building a gaol in the district of Edenton has proved deficient, and the monies in the hands of the commissioners have been all expended in purchasing materials for the same:

I. Be it therefore Enacted by the General Assembly of the State of North Carolina, and it is hereby Enacted by the authority of the same, That each and every hundred acres of land in the county of Chowan shall be subject to a tax of four pence, each poll to a tax of one shilling, and each hundred pounds value of town property to a tax of one shilling: And there shall also be collected in the counties of Tyrrel, Bertie, Perquimans, Pasquotank, Cambden, Currituck, Hertford and Gates, the sum of two pence on every hundred acres of land, and a tax of six pence on every poll, and on every hundred pounds value of town property a tax of six pence in the said counties, to be collected for the year 1786 at the time and in the manner the public taxes are collected for that year; which tax of four pence on every hundred acres of land, and of one shilling on every poll, and of one shilling on every hundred pounds value of taxable property in the county of Chowan, and in the counties of Bertie, Tyrrel, Perquimans, Pasquotank, Cambden, Currituck, Hertford and Gates, the sum of two pence on every hundred acres of land, the sum of six pence on every poll, and on each hundred pounds value of town property the sum of six pence, shall also be levied and collected for the year 1787, in the same manner and at the same time the public taxes laid by the present General Assembly are collected.

II. And be it further Enacted, That the sheriffs of each county shall account with the commissioners appointed for building the said gaol under the same penalties and restrictions as for public taxes, and pay the money into their hands for the purposes aforesaid; which payment shall be allowed them in the settlement of their accounts. (Passed Jan. 6, 1787.)

Appendix B:
Major Officials
of Chowan County

Major Officials of Chowan County

Sheriff

1739	Thomas Luten	1854	Peter F. White
1741	William Luten	1863	William Shannonhouse
1743	Peter Payne	1864	John Norwell
1745	John Alston	1865	F. N. Bond
1747	Joseph Herron	1866	Miles C. Brinkley
1749	John Halsey	1868	Allen C. Ward
1751	John Benbury		Miles C. Brinkley
1752	Peter Payne	1870	William C. Britt
1755	Charles Blount		Miles C. Brinkley
1758	William Halsey	1876	James Manning
1763	Joseph Blount	1878	Miles C. Brinkley
1767	Thomas Bonner	1879	Joseph C. Warren
1769	Thomas Benbury	1880	O. F. Gilbert
1772	James Blount		Joseph C. Warren
1774	John Smith	1888	J. H. Perry
1777	Evan Skinner	1892	L. W. Parker
1780	Edmund Blount	1896	A. Q. Elliot
1789	William Roberts	1900	J. C. Thompson
1795	Charles Roberts	1901	E. S. Norman
1807	William Roberts	1914	George W. Goodwin
	Myles O'Malley,	1932	C. A. Boyce
	Edmund Hoskins	1935	J. Alva Bunch
1808	Edmund Hoskins	1958	Earl Goodwin
1815	James R. Bent	1969	Troy Toppin
1825	William Rascoe	1986	Glenn Perry
1844	Thomas S. Hoskins		

Clerk — What follows is a list which begins with the Clerks of the Chowan County Court of Pleas and Quarter Sessions from 1753 to 1868. That Court was abolished in 1868 and replaced by the Superior Court, Clerks of which are named for the years 1868 to the present. Prior to 1753 James Craven was often named as Clerk, but which Chowan Court he was associated with is unclear.

1753	William Halsey	1841	Thomas V. Hathaway
1755	Thomas Jones	1849	William R. Skinner
1760	(Joseph Herron claims position	1868	Charles E. Robinson
	contesting Jones' appointment.		William R. Skinner
	Jones retains position.)	1885	John C. Bond
1777	James Blount	1891	H. C. Privott
1794	Elisha Norfleet	1906	C. W. Coffield
1811	James Norfleet	1910	F. W. Hobbs
1815	William Norfleet	1922	Richard Dillard Dixon

1820	Henry Wills	1941	E. W. Spires
1828	Edmund Hoskins	1958	Thomas H. Shepard
1837	Thomas V. Hathaway	1961	Lena Leary
	John Bush	1983	Marjorie Hollowell

Register of Deeds

1762	William Halsey	1844	William Wilder
1763	Arthur Howe	1852	Nathan J. Perkins
1769	Alexander Galletly	1870	Oliver F. Gilbert
1777	James Blount	1874	John F. Clayton
1786	James Sutton (Luten?)	1876	Alfred Moore
1793	Thomas Seaman	1881	T. M. Small
1795	William Baines	1892	T. D. Bynum
1810	James Sutton	1896	M. A. Hughes
1817	James Moffatt	1900	T. D. Bynum
1833	Edwin Bond	1906	W. J. Berryman
1835	John Spencer	1910	R. W. Boyce
1837	James Gorham	1924	M. L. Bunch
1838	Thomas J. Charleton	1957	Bertha Bunch
1841	Thomas C. Whidbee	1976	Anna Spruill

Other Officials of Chowan County

(These lists may, in many cases, be incomplete.)

Clerk and Master of Equity

1800	Alexander Millen
1814	John B. Blount
1827	Thomas M. Blount
1829	George Blair
1834	Robert T. Paine
1839	Stephen Elliot
1849	Thomas C. Manning
1855	Joseph Manning
1867	Augustus M. Moore
1868	Court and position abolished

Coroner

1774	John Smith	1880	P. F. White
1786	John Mare	1881	D. M. Lee
1818	Thomas Vail	1884	C. M. Murden
1823	James V. Hathaway	1887	Dr. Thomas Leary
1835	William McNider	1889	A. J. Bateman
1840	Alexander Cheshire	1890	T. S. McMullan
1843	John G. Hankins	1891	J. A. Harris
1856	Edward Warren	1898	J. D. Bullock
1863	Cleveland Sawyer	1899	T. J. Hoskins
1865	W. Rogerson	1907	D. Cason (Position changes to Health
1870	Barclay E. Hults		officer or Superintendent of Board of
1874	Charles E. Robinson		Health.)

County Trustee

1811	Nathaniel Bond
1815	James R. Creecy
1824	William Norcom
1827	Jonathan H. Houghton
1853	Thomas Hudgins
1866	John M. Jones

County Treasurer (Co. Tr.) or Commissioner/Treasurer of Public Building (CPB)

1796	Jacob Blount (CPB)	1884	A. J. Bateman (Co. Tr.)
1800	Elisha Norfleet (Co. Tr.)	1885	K. R. Pendleton (Co. Tr.)
1801	James Hathaway (CPB)	1892	C. S. Vann (Co. Tr.)
1805	Elisha Norfleet (CPB)	1895	B. H. Elliott (Co. Tr.)
1823	Henry Wills (CPB)		C. S. Vann (Co. Tr.)
1826	James Bozman (CPB)	1896	B. H. Elliott (Co. Tr.)
1829	Joseph Manning (CPB)	1898	Z. W. Evans (Co. Tr.)
1834	Edmund Hoskins (CPB)	1908	F. W. White (Co. Tr.)
1837	William D. Rascoe (CPB)	1910	T. E. White
1856	P. F. White (CPB)	1918	W. H. Ward
1876	D. M. Lee (Co. Tr.)	1930	George C. Hoskins
	K. R. Pendleton (Co. Tr.)		

County Solicitor

1797	John Hamilton
1810	James Iredell Jr.
1826	Samuel T. Sawyer
1838	George Satterfield
1841	Thomas G. Houghton
1845	Robert T. Paine
1846	Lucius Johnson
	George Bruer
1852	William C. Hunter
1855	Elias Hines
1857	John S. Hawks

Jailer — Especially in the early years this may have been a temporary job appointed as needed. Much later, this became a duty of the deputy sheriff.

1754	John McKildoe	1864	T. K. Feagan
1768	John Smith	1870	Richard Keogh
	James Sanders	1873	J. Z. Pratt
1769	John Smith	1883	T. M. Harris
1787	William Murray	1893	J. H. Robinson
1788	Henderson Luten	1900	T. P. Leary
1791	Henry Cheshire	1928	W. C. Moore
1819	Abraham Howitt	1929	J. W. Story
1837	William Rea	1933	Sheldon W. Moore
1844	James R. Lemett	1940's	H. F. White
1848	James Floyd	1960's	Glenn Perry
1853	Christopher Rea		

Footnotes

A few important abbreviations are used throughout these notes:

A&H — Division of Archives and History, Raleigh, North Carolina

SHC — Southern Historical Collection, University of North Carolina, Chapel Hill, North Carolina

UNC-CH — University of North Carolina, Chapel Hill, North Carolina

Abbreviated designations for some of the collections held by the Division of Archives and History in Raleigh include the following:

CCR — Colonial Court Records

PRO — Public Records Office (British)

CO — Colonial Office

GO — Governor's Orders

Full bibliographic information will be provided for each initial citation of all works. Subsequent references will appear in an abbreviated form.

Chapter One

1. Clark, Walter L., ed., *State Records of North Carolina*, 16 volumes, (Winston and Goldsboro, State of North Carolina, 1895–1906), Vol. 23, p.95. Hereafter identified in the form *S.R.* 23, p. 95.

2. Hoffman, Margaret M., comp., *Province of North Carolina Abstracts of Land Patents*, [Patent Listing 504, p.179 Patent Book 1], (Weldon, N.C., Roanoke News Co., 1979), p.46.

3. *S.R.* 25, p.175

4. *Chowan County Deed Book B*, p. 232, Edenton, N.C.

5. *S.R.* 25 p.168.

6. Parker, Mattie Erma Edwards; Price,William S.; Cain, Robert J.; editors, *The Colonial Records of North Carolina*, Second Series, 7 Volumes, (Raleigh, N.C., Division of Archives and History, 1963-1984), Vol. 5 p, xix. Hereafter indicated in the form C.R. 2nd 5 p. xix.

7. *Chowan County Deed Book C-1*, Pt. 2 (at end of volume), p. 36, Edenton, North Carolina.

8. *S.R.* 25, pp.175–178.

9. *S.R.* 25, pp. 191–193, sections VI and X.

10. *C.R.* 2nd 5 pp. xiii, xiv, 104.

11. Ibid., p.104.

12. Ibid., p. 125.

13. *Chowan County Deed Book W*, p. 62

14. Ibid., p.125 to 158.

15. Ibid., p. 170.

16. *Chowan County Deed Book B*, p. 620; also *Chowan County Wills*, William Branch, A&H, Raleigh, North Carolina.

17. Compiled from *C.R.* 2nd 5 .

18. *Chowan County Court Minutes, Court of Pleas and Quarter Sessions*, April 1716, A&H, Raleigh, North Carolina. Hereafter indicated by *Chowan Co. Ct. Minutes*; also, in Hathaway J.R.B., *North Carolina Historical and Genealogical Register*, (Edenton, N.C., 1900–1903), Vol I, p. 148.

19. Compiled from *C.R.* 2nd 5.

20. *C.R.* 2nd 5, p. 76; also *Governor's Orders (GO)* 111, p.165, A&H, Raleigh, North Carolina.

21. Original at Old Chowan County Courthouse, Edenton, North Carolina. copy - *Chowan County Miscellaneous Records*, Box 34, A&H, Raleigh, N.C.

22. Byrd, Willliam, *Histories of the Dividing Line Betwixt Virginia and North Carolina*, Reprint of 1929 edition, (New York, Dover Publications, 1967), p. 96.

23. *S.R.* 23, pp. 100–102.

24. *Chowan County Deed Book C – 1* (part 2 at end of volume), p. 35.

25. *Chowan County Deed Book W*, p. 302.

26. *S.R. 25*, p.178 (1722), refers to when "there shall be a Council Room and Gaol built in said town."; and *C.R.* 2nd 7, pp.137–144 (GO 111, p. 306–316).

27. *C.R.* 2nd 7, p.537 "A warrant to Administer oaths to Publick Officers."(GO 110).

28. *C.R.* 2nd 7, p.144 (GO 111, p. 317).

29. Paschal, Herbert R., "Proprietary North Carolina: A study in Colonial Government," unpublished Ph.D. dissertation UNC–CH, 1961, p. 606.

30. Saunders, William L., ed, *Colonial Records of North Carolina*, 10 Volumes, (Raleigh, N.C., State of North Carolina, 1886–1890), Vol 4, pp. 550 and 573. Hereafter indicated in the form, *C.R.* 4 p.550, 573.

31. *Chowan County Accounts*, A&H, Raleigh, North Carolina. "Thomas Barker Esq. in Acc't with Gilbert Leigh," 1758.

32. *Chowan Co. Ct. Minutes*, July 1760.

33. Ibid., May 1763.

34. *C.R.* 2nd 7, p.309, 25 October 1726, ". . . on or about 9 April 1726 did committ to the Publick Goale at Edenton, Ann Speir."

35. *CCR (Colonial Court Records)*, Box 192, "Folder: Public Buildings 1737", A&H Raleigh, North Carolina.

36. *British Records*, PRO (Public Records Office), CO (Colonial Office) 5/333, p. 27–27b, A&H, Raleigh, North Carolina

37. *S.R.* 23, p. 181.

38. Haun, Weynette P., Comp., *Chowan County, N.C. Court Minutes Pleas and Quarter Sessions*, 2 Vols., (Durham, North Carolina, Haun, 1983 and 1984.) Vol I, page 93; text 197, July 1744.

39. Ibid., Vol. II, p. 99; text 165, April 1747.

40. *Chowan County Deed Book C–1*, p. 170.

41. *Chowan County Accounts*, "William Arkile to me Lawrence B. Landerkin", 19 June 1746.

42. *C.R.* 2, p. 604. This document places the records as of 1 January 1725(6). Before being moved to the courthouse, the records were kept in private homes, also a precarious situation. As late as 26 December 1718, the public records were kept at N.C. Deputy Secretary John Lovick's house at Sandy Point. On that date, several men led by Edward Moseley broke into Lovick's house and searched the records looking for evidence af Governor Eden's complicity with pirates.

43. *S.R.* 23, p. 252–267.

44. Following Ms. Haun's practice, I have have indicated the year of either January or February of any given year through the early/mid 1700's in this form. At this time the calendar year began in March, thus what we would call January 1746 was referred to by contemporaries as being in the year 1745.

45. Fries, Adelaide, ed., *Records of the Moravians in North Carolina*, Vol. 1, "Bishop Spangenberg's Diary," (Raleigh, N.C., N.C. Historical Commission, 1922), p. 31–32.

46. Parramore, Thomas, *Cradle of the Colony: The History of Chowan County and Edenton, N.C.*, (Edenton, N.C., Edenton Chamber of Commerce, 1967), pp. 19 -20. "In the last half of 1729 more than sixty vessels cleared Edenton . . ." Also an oft-quoted statistic appearing in Banks and Moore, "History in Towns Edenton, N.C.", in *Antiques*, (June 1979), p.1252: "From 1771 to 1776, 827 ships cleared port at Edenton."

47. See, Powell, Diana, "Artisans in the Colonial South, Chowan County 1714–1776", M.A. thesis, UNC-CH, p. 198.

48. Haun, Vol. I, p. 69; text 153, July 1743.

49. Ibid., Vol. I, P. 75; text 164, October 1743.

50. Hathaway, J.R.B., *N.C. Historical and Genealogical Register*, Vol. II, p. 198.

51. *Chowan Co. Ct. Minutes*, October 1749–July 1753.

52. *Chowan Co. Ct. Minutes*, April 1756.

53. Ibid., November 1756.

54. Ibid., April 1757.

55. Ibid., October 1758.

56. *Chowan County Accounts*, "Work done by Humphrey Robinson for the Prison by Order of the Justices of Chowan County on the Bench then sitting in Edenton," 1751.

57. *Chowan County Accounts*, "Chowan County with Joseph Blount," 1764–1767.

58. Compiled from, Fouts, Raymond P., *Vestry Minutes of St. Paul's Parish Chowan County, N.C. 1701–1776*, (Cocoa, Fla., GenRec Books, 1984).

59. *Chowan County Accounts*, "Work done by Humphrey Robinson for the Prison by Order of the Justices of Chowan County on the Bench then sitting in Edenton," 1751 (The work done on the courthouse was added to the end of the account).
Also, *Chowan Co. Ct. Minutes*, October 1751. ". . . for repairing the courthouse windows. . . ."

60. *Chowan Co. Ct. Minutes*, July 1753.

61. *S.R. 25*, p. 341.

62. *Chowan County Accounts*, "Chowan County in Acc't with Joseph Blount," 1757.

63. *Chowan Co. Ct. Minutes*, October 1760.

64. Ibid., May 1763.

65. Ibid., April and July 1764, and *Chowan County Accounts*, "Chowan County in Acc't with Joseph Blount," 1764–1767.

66. *S.R. 23*, p. 683.

67. *Chowan Co. Ct. Minutes*, October 1766.

68. Haun, Vol. I; text 251, October 1745. As to the spelling of the word "goal"/gaol, the word often appears in Chowan County Records as "goal." Therefore, in direct quotations from documents the spelling used in those documents will be reproduced.

69. Ibid., Vol I, p. 135; text 260, January 1745(46).

70. *Chowan County Accounts*, "Account with Gilbert Leigh," 25 December 1767; "Account Joseph Blount to John van dusey," 1769.

Chapter Two

1. *S.R. 23*, pp. 483–483, 1758.

2. *S.R. 23*, pp. 683–684, 1766.

3. Original at Old Chowan County Courthouse; also, *Chowan County Miscellaneous Records*, Box 34, A&H, Raleigh, North Carolina; also, Hathaway, J.R.B., *N.C. Historical and Genealogical Register*, Vol. II, p. 225.

4. *John Hawks Papers*, UNC-CH, SHC.

5. *British Records*, PRO CO 5/300, pp. 120–122b, A&H, Raleigh, North Carolina.

6. *British Records*, PRO CO 5/300, pp. 115-116b. Letter from Gov. Tryon to Lord Shelbourne, 7 March 1768. (See also, *Correspondence of William Tryon*, William S. Powell. ed., Raleigh, N.C., Division of Archives and History, 1980-81, p. 41.) "The representation in my speech of a Necessity of a stricter Enquiry into the Public Funds ... to inspect into and be informed of the...Public Money."

7. *Chowan Co. Ct. Minutes*, April 1767.

8. Ibid., June 1775.

9. Ibid., September 1778.

10. Ibid., June 1775.

11. Waite, Diana S., "Roofing for Early America," *Building in Early America*, Charles E. Peterson, ed., (Radnor, Pa., Chilton Book Editions, 1976), p.138.

12. Quoted from "William Logan's Journal of a Journey to Georgia 1745", *Pennsylvania Magazine of History and Biography 36*, 1912, in Fenn and Wood, *Natives and Newcomers*, 1912, (Raleigh, N.C., N.C. Dept. of Cultural Resources), p. 31.

13. *Cupola House Papers*, UNC-CH, SHC, microfilm, Reel 2, "Account of Commissioners of the Town of Edenton."

14. Parramore, Thomas, "A History of Chowan County," *Chowan Herald Anniversary Edition*, 18 April 1965, p. 7.

15. *C.R. 7*, p.164; and Fouts, Raymond, *Vestry Minutes of St. Paul's Parish*, 23 May 1767.

16. Hune, Ivor, ed., *Papers in Archeology*, Vol. I, "Five Artifact Studies", (Williamsburg, Va., Colonial Williamsburg Foundation, 1973), p. 80.

17. The existence of the stone floor was described by Architect Frank Benton while doing work on the courthouse for Chowan County. Reported in *Chowan Herald*, 9 October 1947.

18. *Chowan Co. Ct. Minutes*, June 1774.

19. Ibid., June 1768.

20. Loundsbury, Carl, "Order in the Court," unpublished report, Arch. Research Dept., Williamsburg, Va., Colonial Williamsburg, October 1985, pp.44ff.

21. *Chowan Co. Ct. Minutes*, December 1784.

22. Ibid., June 1783.

23. Ibid., June 1791.

24. *Chowan Co. Accounts*, "Jno. Hamilton for the Court House of Edenton," 9 February 1793.

25. Lefler, H.T., and Powell William S., *Colonial North Carolina—A History*, (New York, Charles Scribners and Sons, 1973), p. 167.

26. John Green, partner of Gilbert Leigh, carpenter and house carpenter, is noted in the *Chowan Co. Ct. Minutes* for July 1764 as having erected a house 35' x 18' on town lots 28 and 29 which belonged to James Luten.

27. *Chowan Co. Accounts*, "County of Chowan in acc't with Leigh/Green," 20 September 1770.

28. *Chowan Co. Accounts*, "Chowan Co. to Gilbert Leigh," 4 October 1770.

29. *Chowan Co. Ct. Minutes*, June 1772; and *Chowan Co. Accounts*, "County of Chowan in Acc't with Gilbert Leigh," 12 October 1771.

30. *Chowan Co. Ct. Minutes*, December 1794.

31. *Chowan Co. Accounts*, "State Against Wm. Burke December term 1805."

32. *Chowan Co. Ct. Minutes*, June 1783.

33. *John Shute Papers*, UNC-CH, SHC, "Typescript of Lodge Minutes," 6 July 1778.

34. *S.R. 24*, p. 238, 1778.

35. *Chowan Co. Ct. Minutes*, March 1779.

36. Ibid., June 1779.

37. *Chowan County Miscellaneous Records*, Box 35, A&H, Raleigh, North Carolina.

38. *Cupola House Papers*, Reel 2, "Agreeable to an order September court last ordering us to call on Commissioners for building a goal in Edenton in order to know what sums of money they have in their hands for that purpose which we have and have collected from them the account as follows: . . . J. Beasley, Jos. Underhill, W. Boritz."; and "An Acount of Monies rec'd for the Edenton Goal tax," 1779–1783, presented 8 November 1785, Michael Payne.

39. *S.R. 24*, p. 453.

40. *Chowan Co. Ct. Minutes*, September 1784.

41. Ibid., June 1785.

42. Ibid., December 1787.

43. Ibid., September 1787.

44. Ibid., December 1787.

45. *Cupola House Papers*, Reel 2, "Acc't of the Commissioners of the Town of Edenton."

46. *Chowan Co. Ct. Minutes*, March 1784.

47. Ibid., December 1774.

48. *Cupola House Papers*, Reel 2, "Joshua Bodley Esq. to John Rombough," 1769–1773.

49. *Chowan Co. Ct. Minutes*, October 1767, June 1770; and *Chowan County Accounts*, "Chowan County to John Rombough," 1770.

50. *Chowan County Accounts*, "County of Chowan in Acc't with Thomas Benbury, Sheriff," 1769–1773.

51. *John Shute Papers*, UNC-CH, SHC, 2 January 1776.

52. *Chowan County Miscellaneous Papers*, Vol. 12, "Thomas Williams to James Harrison," September 1767; Vol. 13, reference to Michael Welch, bricklayer; Vol. 14, reference to Nathan Culler, bricklayer, 27 April 1767. *Chowan Co. Ct. Minutes*, Reference to John Elliss, Blacksmith, working on the Public Goal, June 1772; Reference to John Garrett, Blacksmith, working on the Public Goal, June 1772; Reference to John Weir, Blacksmith, working on Public Goal, December 1772, A&H, Raleigh, North Carolina. *Chowan County Accounts*, "County of Chowan to John Elliss," 1770; "County of Chowan to John Elliss," 1771.

53. *Chowan Co. Ct. Minutes*, June 1777.

54. *Chowan Co. Miscellaneous Papers*, Vol. 15.

55. *Chowan Co. Ct. Minutes*, December 1778.

56. Fouts, Raymond, *Vestry Minutes of St. Paul's Parish*, 28 August 1773, 18 May 1774.

57. *Fisherman and Farmer*, 2 October 1891.

58. Higginbotham, Don, ed. and intro., *Papers of James Iredell 1767–1783*, (Raleigh, N.C.

Division of Archives and History, 1976), p. xli.

59. *State Gazette of North Carolina*, 19 February 1789.

60. Ibid., 3 November 1788.

61. Dillard, Richard, in *Fisherman and Farmer Special Edenton Edition*, June 1895; also *Carolina Magazine*, "Edenton Rich in Colonial History," June 1933.

62. Lefler, H.T. and Powell, William S., *Colonial North Carolina—A History*, Scribners, p. 267.

63. Higginbotham, *Papers of James Iredell 1767–1783*, p. xxxviii.

64. *Cupola House Papers*, Reel 2, "Minutes of Public Mass Meeting," 1797; and *Chowan County Accounts*, ". . . cash paid to Henry Wills for inserting in the Gazette the presentment of the Grand Jury reprobating the conduct of the Quakers," December 1796.

65. Maag, Howard, ed., *Journal of Joseph Pilmore*, (Philadelphia, Historical Society of the Philadelphia Annual Conference of the United Methodist Church, 1969 reprint), pp. 170–171.

66. Lee, Leroy, *Life and Times of the Reverend Jesse Lee*, (Richmond, Va., John Early for the Methodist Episcopal Church South, 1898), pp. 105–107; and Thrift, Minton, ed., *Memoir of the Reverend Jesse Lee*, (New York, N. Bangs and T. Mason for the M.E. Church, 1823), pp. 45-48.

67. Clark, Elmer, ed., *Journals and Letters of Francis Asbury*, (London, Epworth Press, 3 Vols., 1958), Vol. I, pp. 450-451.

68. Ibid., Vol. II, p. 407.

69. Ibid., Vol. II, pp. 495-496.

70. Quoted in Grissom, W.L., *History of Methodism in North Carolina*, (Nashville, Tn., Smith and Lamar, 1905), p. 341, from Coke's Diary printed in *Arminian Magazine*, 1789.

71. Johnston, Hugh Buckner, ed., "Journal of Ebenezer Hazard," *North Carolina Historical Review*, 1959, p. 365.

72. Ibid., p. 362.

73. Wright, Louis B. and Tinling, Marion, ed., *Quebec to Carolina 1785–1786 Being the Observations of Robert Hunter Jr. Young Merchant of London*, (San Marino, Ca., Huntington Library, 1943), pp. 266 -267.

74. *Chowan Co. Ct. Minutes*, September 1769.

75. *Chowan County Accounts*," County of Chowan in Acc't with Thomas Benbury Sheriff."

76. *Chowan Co. Ct. Minutes*, March 1781.

77. Ibid., September 1781.

78. *S.R.* 25, pp. 455-456.

79. *Chowan County Miscellaneous Records*, Box 35, A&H, Raleigh, North Carolina; and *Chowan Co. Ct. Minutes*, December 1790.

80. *S.R.* 24, pp. 873–874.

81. *Chowan Co. Ct. Minutes*, December 1790.

82. *Cupola House Papers*, Reel 2, "Dr. the District Jail of Edenton to Nathaniel Allen one of the Commissioners for Building the Same."

83. Ibid., "Dr. the District Jail of Edenton to Joseph Blount one of the Commissioners for Building the Same."

84. *Chowan Co. Ct. Minutes*, December 1789.

85. *State Gazette*, 26 February 1789.

86. *Chowan Co. Ct. Minutes*, September 1794.

87. *Chowan County Accounts*, "Account to Jacob Blount," 1795.

88. *S.R.* 24, p.452.

89. Wright, Louis B., ed., *Quebec to Carolina . . .*, p. 267.

90. *Cupola House Papers*, Reel 3, "Samuel Lattimore rec'd of Samuel Standin Town Commissioner," 17 December 1789.

91. *Chowan County Accounts*, "Commissioners of the Town of Edenton Account with John Little, Town Treasurer," 1796.

92. For more information see, Bishir, Catherine, "Black Builders in Antebellum North Carolina," *North Carolina Historical Review*, October 1984.

93. *Chowan County Accounts*, "Commissioners of the Town of Edenton Account with John Little, Town Treasurer," 1796.

94. *Chowan Co. Ct. Minutes*, February 1861.

95. *David Swain Papers*, A & H, Raleigh, North Carolina.

Chapter Three

1. *Chowan Co. Ct. Minutes*, March 1806.
2. *Cupola House Papers*, Reel 3, "Commissioners of the Town of Edenton by order of Mr. Millen to William Nichols."
3. *Cupola House Papers*, Reel 3, "Commissioners of Edenton to Alexander Millen."
4. *Cupola House Papers*, Reel 3, "Commissioners of Edenton to Alexander Millen," and "Commissioners of Edenton to Henry King."
5. *Cupola House Papers*, Reel 3, "Commissioners of Edenton to Matthew Sawyer."
6. *Cupola House Papers*, Reel 3, "Commissioners of Edenton to John Little, their Treasurer."
7. *Cupola House Papers*, Reel 3, "Commissioners of Edenton to Alexander Millen."
8. *Cupola House Papers*, Reel 3, "Commissioners of the Town of Edenton to William Nichols." Unfortunately the last page(s) of this account is missing.
9. *Cupola House Papers*, Reel 3, "James Hathaway Esq. to Welcome Mason."
10. *Chowan Co. Ct. Minutes*, June 1816; also *Cupola House Papers*, Reel 3.
11. *Chowan Co. Ct. Minutes*, December 1816; and *Chowan County Orders of the Court of Pleas and Quarter Sessions* – A, microfilm, A&H, Raleigh, North Carolina.
12. *Chowan County Accounts*, "County of Chowan in account with J.R. Creecy, Trustee," December 1817; "County of Chowan in account with J.R. Creecy, Trustee," September 1818.
13. *Cupola House Papers*, Reel 3, "Terms upon which Court House steeple is to be let to lowest bidder."
14. Ibid.
15. *Chowan Co. Ct. Minutes*, September 1826; also, *Henry Wills Account Book*, A&H, Raleigh, North Carolina.
16. *Cupola House Papers*, Reel 5, "Edmund Hoskins to Mr. Bingham," 1826.
17. *Cupola House Papers*, Reel 5, "Edmund Hoskins to N. Howcott," 1828.
18. *Cupola House Papers*, Reel 3, "Commissioners of Edenton to Edward Brown," 1846.
19. *American Banner*, 18 May 1856.
20. *Cupola House Papers*, Reel 3, "Commissioners of Edenton to Henry King"; and *Chowan County Accounts*, "Mr. Nathaniel Bond County Trustee to John Little."
21. *Cupola House Papers*, Reel 3, "Commissioners of Edenton to Alexander Millen."
22. *Cupola House Papers*, Reel 3, "Nathaniel Bond County Trustee In Acc't with the County of Chowan."
23. *Chowan Co. Ct. Minutes*, March 1826.
24. Ibid., June 1832.
25. *Chowan County Accounts*, "Edmund Hoskins, For the Court House to David Dickerson."
26. *Chowan Co. Ct. Minutes*, June 1833.
27. Ibid., May 1834.
28. *Chowan County Accounts*, "The County of Chowan in Acc't with J.R. Creecy, Trustee," December 1817.
29. *Chowan County Accounts*, "The County of Chowan in Acc't with J.R. Creecy, Trustee," September 1818.
30. Regarding: Nichols and Baptist Meeting House – *Cupola House Papers*, Reel 2 and Reel 4; Nichols and apprentice – *Chowan Co. Ct. Minutes*, September 1807; Nichols and petition for naturalization – *Chowan Co. Minutes*, December 1813.
31. *Edenton Gazette*, 7 July 1829.
32. *Chowan County Accounts*, "Chowan County to Hezikiah Gorham," 1812.
33. Ibid.
34. *Chowan Co. Ct. Minutes*, December 1826.
35. *Chowan County Accounts*, March 1809.
36. *Chowan County Accounts*, "Edmund Hoskins to Gus A. Johnson," 1835.
37. *Cupola House Papers*, Reel 3, "Commissioners of Edenton to William Nichols," 1807.
38. *Elisha Norfleet's Letters and Accounts*, A&H, Raleigh, North Carolina; also, *Chowan Co. Ct. Minutes*, June 1807.
39. *Chowan Co. Ct. Minutes*, December 1810; also, *Chowan County Accounts*, "To James Sutton, Register," 1810.
40. *Chowan Co. Ct. Minutes*, December 1810; also, *Chowan County Accounts*, "J.B. Blount to Wm. Manning."
41. *Chowan Co. Ct. Minutes*, June 1829.
42. Ibid., December 1830.

43. *Edenton Gazette*, 26 January 1827.

44. *Chowan Co. Ct. Minutes*, March 1827.

45. Ibid., June 1828.

46. Ibid., December 1824.

47. Ibid., June 1825.

48. Ibid., December 1824.

49. *Edenton Gazette*, 7 July 1808.

50. Ibid., 29 February 1809.

51. Ibid., 21 July 1808 and 15 September 1808.

52. Ibid., 9 November 1810.

53. *James Norcom Papers*, "Letter to his son John, 14 June 1819," A&H, Raleigh, North Carolina

54. *Edenton Gazette*, 11 November 1828.

55. Ibid., 12 October 1810.

56. Ibid., 6 April 1819.

57. Ibid., 13 April 1819.

58. *Chowan Co. Ct. Minutes*, September 1807 and March 1808; and *Chowan County Miscellaneous Records*, Box 35, A&H, Raleigh, North Carolina.

59. *General Assembly Session Records*, November and December 1807, A&H, Raleigh, North Carolina.

60. *Chowan Co. Ct. Minutes*, June 1808.

61. *Chowan County Accounts*, "To the Worshipful County Court of Chowan from Collins, Little, and Hathaway," 17 June 1807.

62. *Edenton Gazette*, 20 January 1809.

63. *Chowan County Accounts*, "The Commissioners for Building a Jail in Edenton in Acc't with John Little their Treasurer."

64. *Edenton Gazette*, 25 August, 1809.

65. *Chowan County Accounts*, "The Commissioners for Building a Jail in Edenton in Acc't with John Little their Treasurer."

66. *Chowan Co. Ct. Minutes*, September 1810.

67. *Chowan County Accounts*, "The Commissioners for Building a Jail in Edenton in Acc't with John Little their Treasurer."

68. Ibid.

69. *Chowan Co. Ct. Minutes*, September 1815.

70. Ibid., September 1818.

71. *Chowan County Accounts*, "The Commissioners for Building a Jail in Edenton in Acc't with John Little their Treasurer."

72. *Chowan Co. Ct. Minutes*, September 1815.

73. *Orders of the Court of Pleas and Quarter Sessions*, Chowan County, "Trustees for the County of Chowan to John Littlejohn," 1811–1814, microfilm, A&H, Raleigh, North Carolina.

74. Ibid., "James R. Bent to Edmund Hoskins for the Jail," 28 August 1817.

75. *Chowan County Accounts*, "Chowan Co. to Abe Howitt," 1819.

76. *Chowan Co. Ct. Minutes*, September 1820 and June 1821.

77. *Chowan County Accounts*, "Account to John Standin," 24 July 1825.

78. *Chowan Co. Ct. Minutes*, June 1812; and *Chowan Co. Ct. Minutes*, early 1820's.

79. *Orders of the Court of Pleas and Quarter Sessions*, Chowan County, "Chowan Co. to J.R. Bent," 17 August 1817, microfilm, A&H, Raleigh, North Carolina.

80. *Chowan County Accounts*, "Chowan County to Josiah Collins," 31 July 1819.

81. Ibid.; and *Chowan Co. Ct. Minutes*, September 1819.

82. *Chowan Co. Ct. Minutes*, September 1819.

83. Ibid., June 1819.

84. Ibid., June 1822.

85. The entire paragraph to this point is from *Chowan Co. Ct. Minutes*, December 1824.

86. *Chowan Co. Ct. Minutes*, March 1826.

87. Ibid., September 1825.

88. *Chowan County Accounts*, "Chowan Co. to Wm. Norcom, Co. Trustee," 27 July 1825.

89. *Chowan County Estates*, Ebenezer Paine, A&H, Raleigh, North Carolina.

90. Ibid.

91. Ibid.

92. *Third Census of the United States*, North Carolina, 1810, A&H, Raleigh, North

Carolina.

93. "Edenton, North Carolina: An Historical and Pictorial Essay," *Southern Antiques and Interiors*, John G. Zehner, Director, Elizabeth Wilborn, Researcher, Division of Historic Sites and Museums, N.C. Office of Archives and History, Fall 1972, p. 8.

94. *First Census of the United States*, North Carolina, 1790, A&H, Raleigh, North Carolina.

95. *Robert T. Paine Papers*, "Letter 28," March 1832, UNC-CH, SHC.

96. *North Carolina State Census*, 1784-1787, A&H, Raleigh, North Carolina.

97. See *Chowan County Deed Book A-3*, "Deed of Trust from Michael Payne to Nathaniel Allen, Samuel Dickerson, John Armistead, Jacob Jordan, and Stephen Cabarrus," 8 May 1799, p. 265.

98. *Chowan Co. Ct. Minutes*, December 1826.

99. *Chowan County Accounts*, "Edmund Hoskins to A. Moore," November 1834.

100. *Chowan Co. Ct. Minutes*, November 1834.

101. Lefler, H.T., ed., *North Carolina History as Told by Contemporaries*, (Chapel Hill, North Carolina, University of North Carolina Press, 1934), p. 267.

102. Parramore, Thomas, "A History of Chowan County," *Chowan Herald Souvenir Edition*, 8 April 1965.

103. *Chowan Co. Ct. Minutes*, September 1831.

104. Ibid., March 1832.

105. *Edenton Gazette*, 7 July 1808. This building, if constructed, would have replaced the building which received repairs in 1796.

106. *Edenton Town Council Minutes*, 28 May 1872, microfilm, A&H, Raleigh, North Carolina.

107. *Cupola House Papers*, Reel 3, "Account of John Littlejohn with the Commissioners of the Town of Edenton."

108. *Edenton Town Council Minutes*, 26 July 1866, microfilm, A&H, Raleigh, North Carolina.

Chapter Four

1. *Chowan Co. Ct. Minutes*, June 1833.

2. *Chowan County Accounts*, "Edmund Hoskins Commissioner of Public Building (CPB) to James C. Johnston," November 1835.

3. *Chowan County Accounts*, "Chowan Co. in Acc't with Commissioner of Public Building Edmund Hoskins, (roofing the Court House with zinc)," 1835.

4. From *Chowan Co. Ct. Minutes*, 1832 to 1836.

5. *Chowan County Accounts*, "An invoice from Houghton, Booth, Boardman, and Noble, N.Y. to Edmund Hoskins, Superintendent of Public Buildings, Chowan County N. C.," 2 December 1835.

6. The above figures from *Chowan County Accounts*, "Chowan Co. in Acc't with CPB Edmund Hoskins," 1835.

7. *Chowan Co. Ct. Minutes*, February 1837.

8. Ibid., February 1838.

9. *James Norcom Papers*, "Letter 23," May 1837, A&H, Raleigh, North Carolina.

10. *Chowan Co. Ct. Minutes*, August 1837. Curiously, at this same August term of Court a last reference in the *Minutes* is made to Edmund Hoskins, one of the men in charge of the first roofing project on the courthouse: ". . . Court proceeded to elect a clerk to fill the vacancy occassioned by the removal out of the state of Edmund Hoskins, former Clerk . . ." Note also that the County Trustee at the time of the project was Jonathan H. Houghton, the contractor for the job.

11. Ibid., November 1837.

12. *Chowan County Accounts*, "County of Chowan to Wm. Rascoe," 1837.

13. *Chowan County Accounts*, "Wm Rascoe Esq. Treasurer of Public Building Chowan Co. to Wm. D. Delaney," 1837.

14. *Chowan Co. Ct. Minutes*, November 1837.

15. *Chowan County Accounts*, "Note to J. Coffield from Wm. Rascoe," 14 November 1837.

16. *Chowan County Accounts*, "Receipt from Wm. Delaney," 15 November 1837.

17. *Chowan Co. Ct. Minutes*, November 1839.

18. Ibid., February 1840.

19. Ibid., May 1840.

20. Ibid., August 1840; also, Henry Wills' *Account Book*, A&H, Raleigh, North Carolina.

21. *Chowan Co. Ct. Minutes*, August 1847.

22. Ibid., August 1848.

23. *Chowan County Miscellaneous Records*, Box 35, Public Buildings File, A&H, Raleigh, North Carolina.

24. *Chowan Co. Ct. Minutes*, November 1848.

25. *Chowan County Accounts*, "Receipt from Spruill and Morse with Thomas S. Hoskins, Sheriff of Chowan County," 25 August 1849.

26. *Chowan Herald*, 25 July 1940.

27. *Chowan County Accounts*, June 1838.

28. *American Banner*, 8 May 1856.

29. *Chowan Co. Ct. Minutes*, March 1858.

30. *Cupola House Papers*, Reel 3, (Court Order ?).

31. Dillard, Richard, *The Civil War in Chowan County*, Raleigh, North Carolina, (North Carolina Historical Commission, 1916), pp. 5-7.

32. Parramore, Thomas, *Cradle of the Colony: The History of Chowan County and Edenton, N.C.*, (Edenton, N.C., Edenton Chamber of Commerce, 1967), pp. 72-73.

33. *Chowan County Accounts*, "Edmund Hoskins with M. Clark for the Court House," 15 June 1836.

34. *Chowan County Accounts*, "Received from Edmund Hoskins, CPB (Commissioner of Public Building)," 20 June 1836.

35. *Chowan County Accounts*, "Chowan Co. in Acc't with Edmund Hoskins, CPB," 1835.

36. *Cupola House Papers*, Reel 3, "Commissioners of Edenton to Matthew Sawyer," October 1806.

37. Ibid., "Commissioners of Edenton by Order of Mr. Millen to William Nichols," 1806.

38. Ibid., "Commissioners of Edenton to John Little their Treasurer," 1808.

39. *Chowan Co. Ct. Minutes*, May 1850.

40. *Chowan County Accounts*, "Edmund Hoskins to Isham Stewart," 1836.

41. *Chowan Co. Ct. Minutes*, August 1860.

42. Ibid., February 1840.

43. Ibid., May 1840.

44. Ibid., May 1842.

45. Ibid.

46. Ibid., August 1844.

47. Ibid., August 1845.

48. Ibid., February 1843.

49. Ibid., November 1846 and February 1856.

50. Ibid., November 1846.

51. Ibid., May 1849.

52. Ibid., November 1850.

53. Ibid., August 1852.

54. Ibid., February 1856.

55. *Chowan County Accounts*, "Commissioner of Public Building of Chowan Co. to Wm Rascoe," February 1838 and February 1839.

56. *Chowan Co. Ct. Minutes*, June 1838.

57. Ibid., August 1853.

58. Ibid., May 1855.

59. Ibid., May 1849.

60. Ibid.

61. Ibid., February 1862.

62. Ibid., August 1865.

63. Ibid., November 1846.

64. Ibid., February 1842.

65. Ibid., October 1842.

66. Ibid., February 1850.

67. Ibid., November 1850.

68. *Chowan County Accounts*, "Chowan Co. to T.S. Hoskins, Sheriff."

69. *Chowan Co. Ct. Minutes*, August 1850.

70. Ibid., February 1852.

71. *Albemarle Bulletin*, 1 May 1850.

72. *Chowan Co. Ct. Minutes*, May 1855.

73. Ibid., February 1856.

74. Garrett, J.H., from "An Historic Sketch of the County of Chowan," *Albemarle Times*, May and June 1871, UNC-CH, North Carolina Collection.

75. Ibid., Garrett gives his article the advantage of an eyewitness perspective, which may at the same time be a disadvantage due to his own role as a participant in a highly political event.

76. *Edenton Town Council Minutes*, 30 September 1866, A&H, Raleigh, North Carolina.

77. Quoted in Parramore's "History of Chowan County," *Chowan Herald Souvenir Edition*, 8 April 1965, p. 9.

78. Ibid.

79. *Chowan Co. Ct. Minutes*, August 1837.

80. *Chowan County Accounts*, "Report of the Grand Jury," 6 August 1860.

81. *Chowan Co. Ct. Minutes*, November 1851.

82. Ibid., August 1837.

83. *Chowan County Accounts*, "Chowan Co. for repairs of Jail and Yard to Wm. Rea," May 1838.

84. *Chowan Co. Ct. Minutes*, November 1842.

85. *Chowan County Accounts*, "Wm. Kirby with Chowan Co.," December 1842.

86. *Chowan Co. Ct. Minutes*, May 1846.

87. Ibid., November 1851.

88. Ibid., August 1852–May 1856.

89. Ibid., August 1859.

90. *Chowan County Accounts*, "T.S. Hoskins to Starkey Perry," paid 20 December 1853.

91. *Chowan County Accounts*, "Chowan Co. to T. S. Hoskins," 1854.

92. *Chowan County Accounts*, "Report of the Grand Jury," 1860.

93. *Chowan Co. Ct. Minutes*, May 1838.

94. *Chowan County Accounts*, "Chowan Co. to T.S. Hoskins," August 1854.

95. *Chowan Co. Ct. Minutes*, February 1861.

96. *Edenton Town Council Minutes*, 24 May 1866, A&H, Raleigh, North Carolina.

Chapter Five

1. Garrett, J.H., "History of the County of Chowan," *Albemarle Times*, May and June 1871, UNC-CH, North Carolina Collection.

2. *American Banner*, 2 October 1856.

3. Mullen quoted in Parramore, "History of Chowan County," *Chowan Herald Souvenir Edition*, 8 April 1965, p. 11.

4. *Chowan Co. Board of Commissioners Minutes*, 6 September 1880, Edenton, North Carolina. (Hereafter simply referred to as *Commissioners Minutes*.)

5. Ibid., 3 December 1883.

6. Ibid., 5 December 1881.

7. Ibid., 6 February 1882; and 4 June 1883 when S.W. Goodwin buys 300 ft. of lumber for $3.

8. Ibid., 1 September 1884.

9. Ibid., 1885.

10. Ibid., 4 June 1885.

11. *Chowan Herald*, 25 July 1940.

12. *Commissioners Minutes*, 4 June 1885.

13. Ibid.

14. *Fisherman and Farmer*, 6 December 1887.

15. Ibid., 5 June 1891.

16. Ibid., 4 September 1891.

17. *Commissioners Minutes*, 5 October 1891.

18. *Fisherman and Farmer*, 23 October 1891.

19. Ibid., 30 October 1891.

20. Ibid.

21. *Commissioners Minutes*, 16 November 1869.

22. Ibid., 4 January 1875.

23. Ibid., 7 May 1877, 7 September 1885, 12 July 1886.

24. Ibid., 1 August 1887, 6 September 1887.

25. Ibid., 3 July 1893.

26. Ibid., 6 June 1881.

27. Ibid., 5 April 1886.

28. Ibid., 3 May 1886.

29. *Fisherman and Farmer*, 13 April 1894; and *Commissioners Minutes*, 3 May 1894.

30. *Commissioners Minutes*, 5 July 1886 and 3 April 1893.

31. Duke University Manuscript Collection, post card file—Chowan County.

32. *Commissioners Minutes*, 9 February 1875.

33. Ibid., 4 April 1881.

34. *Fisherman and Farmer*, 13 April 1894.

35. *Commissioners Minutes*, 3 August 1885.

36. Ibid., 9 February 1875.

37. Ibid., 14 November 1872, 1 February 1886.

38. Ibid., 2 November 1874.

39. Ibid., 3 December 1877, 1 February 1886.

40. Ibid., 3 December 1883.

41. Ibid., 9 February 1875.

42. Ibid., 4 February 1895.

43. Ibid., 5 January 1874.

44. Ibid., 6 December 1886, 6 April 1891.

45. *Fisherman and Farmer*, 9 January 1891.

46. *Commissioners Minutes*, 7 October 1872.

47. Ibid., 7 January 1895.

48. Ibid., 4 February 1895.

49. *Fisherman and Farmer*, 8 April 1892.

50. Ibid.

51. Ibid., 6 July 1885. The rest of the paragraph was culled from the *Commissioners Minutes*.

52. 7 April 1879.

53. *Albemarle Enquirer*, 29 July 1886.

54. *Fisherman and Farmer*, 6 September 1895.

55. Ibid., 25 May 1894.

56. *Commissioners Minutes*, September 1873.

57. Ibid., 6 May 1878.

58. Ibid., 15 October 1877.

59. Ibid., 3 June 1878.

60. Ibid., 7 October 1878.

61. Ibid., 25 November 1878.

62. Ibid., 2 December 1878.

63. Ibid., 7 January 1879.

64. Ibid., 1 October 1879.

65. Ibid., 7 January 1880.

66. Ibid., 4 June 1885.

67. Ibid., 2 November 1885.

68. *Chowan County Orders and Decrees B 1865–1904, Minutes of the County Board of Magistrates*, 11 June 1886, microfilm, A&H, Raleigh, North Carolina.

69. *Commissioners Minutes*, 5 March 1888.

70. Ibid., 2 January 1888.

71. Ibid., 2 April 1888.

72. Ibid., 4 March 1892.

73. Ibid., 4 April 1892.

74. Ibid., 2 July 1894.

75. Ibid., 4 April 1894.

76. Ibid., 1 September 1884.

77. Ibid., 23 July 1883.

78. Ibid., 7 January 1889.

79. Ibid., 5 July 1870.

80. *Edenton Town Council Minutes*, 14 October 1871, microfilm, A&H, Raleigh, North Carolina.

81. *Fisherman and Farmer*, 14 April 1893.

82. *Edenton Town Council Minutes*, 5 December 1893, microfilm, A&H, Raleigh, North Carolina.

83. Ibid., 13 March 1894.

84. Ibid., 28 November 1871 and 28 August 1872.

85. Ibid., 2 January 1872 and 2 February 1876.

86. Ibid., 14 May 1870.

87. *Fisherman and Farmer Special Edition*, 31 October 1890.

88. *Commissioners Minutes*, 4 August 1877 and November 1878.

Chapter Six

1. *Commissioners Minutes*, 2 August 1897.

2. Ibid., 2 August 1897 and 3 January 1898.

3. Ibid., 16 October 1897.

4. Ibid., 6 December 1926.

5. Ibid., 19 June 1947.

6. Ibid., 22 September 1947.

7. *Chowan Herald*, 25 September 1947.

8. Ibid.

9. Ibid., 9 October 1947.

10. Ibid., 23 October 1947.

11. *Commissioners Minutes*, 20 October 1947.

12. *Chowan Herald*, 9 October 1947.

13. *Commissioners Minutes*, 6 June 1904.

14. Ibid., 4 July 1904 and 11 July 1904.

15. Ibid., 1 August 1904.

16. *Eastern Courier*, 25 January 1900.

17. *Commissioners Minutes*, 7 December 1925.

18. Ibid., 1 August 1960.

19. *Chowan Herald*, 19 August 1960.

20. For example, former Board member Dallas Jethro recalls that the building was sand blasted. A Lynn Thomas Co. could not supply any useful information regarding this question.

21. *Commissioners Minutes*, 8 December 1960.

22. Ibid., 5 December 1960.

23. Ibid., 6 February 1961 and 6 March 1961.

24. Ibid., 1 April 1910 and 1 August 1910.

25. Ibid., 2 January 1911.

26. Ibid., 5 February 1912.

27. Ibid., 3 July 1916.

28. Newspaper clipping from North Carolina Collection, UNC-CH, Clipping File, no date, no identification.

29. *Commissioners Minutes*, 7 July 1970.

30. Ibid., 5 February 1971.

31. Ibid., 3 August 1903.

32. Ibid., 5 June 1939.

33. *Chowan Herald*, 10 March 1938.

34. *Commissioners Minutes*, 6 May 1940.

35. *Chowan Herald*, 25 July 1940.

36. *Commissioners Minutes*, 2 February 1954.

37. Ibid., 1 March 1954.

38. Ibid., 6 July 1960.

39. Letter, 16 October 1978 from Larry E. Tise, State Historical Preservation Officer, N.C. Dept. of Cultural Resources, to Henry E. Dick, County Manager, Chowan County, Office of the County Manager, Edenton, North Carolina.

40. Letter, 7 November 1978 from Everette Fauber to Henry E. Dick.

41. Letter, 11 September 1979 from Cliff Copeland, Chowan County Manager, to A.L. Honeycutt, A&H, Office of the County Manager, Edenton, North Carolina.

42. Letter, 11 March 1981, Lloyd D. Childers, Grants in Aid Administrator, to Cliff Copeland, Office of the County Manager, Edenton, North Carolina.

43. *Commissioners Minutes*, 2 June 1913.

44. Ibid., 7 August 1950.
45. *Chowan Herald*, 10 August 1950.
46. *Commissioners Minutes*, 7 November 1960.
47. Ibid., 4 May 1930.
48. Ibid., 5 July 1915.
49. Ibid., 6 December 1943.
50. *Chowan Herald*, 9 December 1943.
51. *Commissioners Minutes*, 3 January 1910.
52. Ibid., 5 May 1924.
53. Ibid., 1 August 1904.
54. Ibid., 7 January 1907.
55. Ibid., 7 September 1907.
56. *Chowan Herald*, 1 August and 8 August 1940.
57. *Commissioners Minutes*, 6 December 1954.
58. Ibid., 3 September 1958.
59. Ibid., 7 December 1925.
60. Ibid., 2 February 1959.
61. Ibid., 7 December 1925.
62. Ibid., 7 March 1949.
63. Ibid., 6 November 1899.
64. Ibid., 2 April 1900. The Special Edenton Edition of the *Fisherman and Farmer*, 31 October 1890, had this to say about Theo Ralph as it discussed contractors and builders in Edenton: "Just here we would say if there is anyone in Edenton that deserves to have his name perpetuated in the town's history, it is Mr. (Theo) Ralph. He came to Edenton about 5 years ago with small means . . . and not only built up an estate, but helped others, too. He had done all in his power to advance Edenton, has constructed a number of fine buildings, and has ornamented our city, as well as having been useful to her." The paper went on to say that Ralph's house on the NE corner of Main and Gale was a George F. Barber design marked by an "octagon shaped tower." By 3 April 1896, the *Fisherman and Farmer* reported that Ralph was building "a factory on Church St. for the manufacture of sash, doors, and blinds." An article from the following month mentioned his sash and door establishment on Broad St.
65. Hathaway, J.R.B., *North Carolina Historical and Genealogical Register*, Vol. I, #2, p. 309.
66. *Eastern Courier*, 25 January 1900.
67. *Commissioners Minutes*, 5 October 1925.
68. *Chowan Herald*, 29 February 1940.
69. *Commissioners Minutes*, 6 September 1909.
70. *Chowan Herald*, 1 December 1949.
71. *Commissioners Minutes*, 5 December 1949.
72. Ibid.
73 Ibid., 6 May 1968.
74. Ibid., 7 September 1931.
75. Ibid., 2 March 1970 and 7 January 1970.
76. Ibid., 7 July 1970.
77. Ibid., 7 November 1906 and 7 January 1907.
78. Ibid., 4 February 1924.
79. Ibid., 3 February 1919.
80. Ibid., 6 January 1925.
81. Ibid., 4 July 1927.
82. Ibid., 3 August 1937.
83. *Chowan Herald*, 24 February 1938.
84. Ibid.
85. *Commissioners Minutes*, 1 February 1937.
86. *Chowan Herald*, 9 October 1947.
87. Ibid., 15 August 1940.
88. *Commissioners Minutes*, 7 November 1966.
89. Ibid., 3 July 1967.
90. Ibid., 6 December 1967.
91. Ibid., 1 March 1909.
92. Ibid., 5 October 1925.
93. Ibid., 10 July 1941.
94. *Chowan Herald*, 7 August 1941.

95. Ibid., 7 October 1943.
96. *Commissioners Minutes*, 1 April 1946.
97. Ibid., 3 April 1953.
98. Ibid., 4 August 1952.
99. Ibid., 4 September 1911 and 3 February 1912.
100. Ibid., 4 September 1911.
101. Ibid., 2 May 1949.
102. Ibid., 7 August 1954.
103. *Chowan Herald*, 10 February 1938.
104. *Commissioners Minutes*, 7 March 1938.
105. Ibid., 7 January 1907 and 4 March 1907.
106. Ibid., 7 February 1921 and 5 January 1942.
107. Interview with Bertha Bunch, former Register of Deeds, March 1986.
108. *Commissioners Minutes*, 7 May 1933.
109. Ibid., 1 April 1947 and 4 April 1949.
110. Ibid., 4 August 1913.
111. Ibid., 2 April 1917.
112. Ibid., 14 July 1919 and 2 May 1921.
113. Ibid., 7 February 1927.
114. *Chowan Herald*, 10 February 1938.
115. *Commissioners Minutes*, 5 February 1940.
116. *Chowan Herald*, 11 July 1940.
117. *Commissioners Minutes*, 3 November 1958 and conversations with Elizabeth Vann Moore, February 1986.
118. *Commissioners Minutes*, 8 September 1961.
119. Ibid., 2 November 1961 and 5 September 1962.
120. *Chowan Herald*, 25 February 1965.
121. *Commissioners Minutes*, 30 May 1918.
122. *Chowan Herald*, 6 August 1942.
123. *Commissioners Minutes*, 19 June 1947.
124. *Chowan Herald*, 28 March 1968.
125. Ibid.
126. *Commissioners Minutes*, 6 April 1970.
127. Ibid., 6 June 1970.
128. *Chowan Herald*, 8 June 1961.
129. Ibid., 3 March 1960.
130. Ibid., 18 May 1961.
131. Ibid., 8 June 1961.
132. *Commissioners Minutes*, 1 August 1905.
133. Ibid., 18 December 1905.
134. Ibid., 7 February 1921.
135. Ibid., 3 February 1919.
136. Ibid., 16 February 1952.
137. Ibid., 10 July 1905.
138. Ibid., 6 November 1905 and 18 December 1905.
139. Ibid., 3 March 1941.
140. Ibid., 5 March 1951.
141. Ibid., 4 November 1935 and 3 September 1952.
142. Ibid., 12 June 1967.
143. Ibid., 6 June 1904.
144. Ibid., 3 August 1939.
145. *News and Observer*, Raleigh, North Carolina, 6 September 1970.
146. *Commissioners Minutes*, 4 June 1906.
147. Ibid., 1 October 1906.
148. Ibid., 7 November 1910 and 6 December 1910.
149. Ibid., 4 August 1913, 4 February 1918, and 4 November 1918.
150. Ibid., 1 April 1912.
151. Ibid., 9 September 1942, 7 May 1945, and 21 May 1945.
152. Ibid., 4 June 1945.
153. Ibid., 14 June 1947.
154. Ibid., 3 November 1958.

155. Ibid., 20 August 1960.
156. Ibid., 2 October 1967.
157. Ibid., 6 October 1969.
158. Ibid., 7 July 1970.
159. Ibid., 3 August 1970.
160. Ibid., 9 October 1970

Concluding Notes

1. "Letter, Governor Tryon to Lord Shelbourne," 7 March 1768, *British Records*, PRO, CO5/300, p.127–131b, [See also *Correspondence of William Tryon*, William S. Powell, ed., p. 42.]

2. Lane, Mills, *Architecture of the Old South*, (Savannah, Georgia, Beehive Press, 1985), p.48.

3. *State Gazette*, 12 November 1790, "Died at New Bern in an advanced age, after a short illness on 31 ultimate John Hawks Esq."

Bibliography

Manuscript Sources

University of North Carolina, Southern Historical Collection, Chapel Hill, North Carolina

Brownrigg Papers
Josiah Collins Papers
Cupola House Papers
Edenton Papers
Family Records (Robert Smith)
Francis Lister Hawks Papers
John Hawks Papers
Hayes Collection
James Iredell Papers
Miscellaneous Collection
Miscellaneous Letters
Robert T. Paine Papers
Pettigrew Papers
John Shute Papers (Masonic Records)

Duke University Manuscript Collection, Durham, North Carolina

Richard Brownrigg Merchant's Ledger
William Badham Jr. Letters and Papers
Josiah Collins Papers
Samuel Dickenson and David Black Papers
Thomas Hathaway Papers
Robert R. Heath Letters and Papers
Edmund Hoskins Papers
James Iredell Papers
Chowan County Postcard Collection

Chowan County Courthouse, Edenton, North Carolina

Chowan County Deed Books
Minutes of the Board of County Commissioners
Records of Wills and Estates

North Carolina State Archives, Raleigh, North Carolina

Account Books including those of William Luten, carpenter; Joseph Harris, blacksmith; and Henry Wills, merchant and County Clerk
Tillie Bond Collection
British Records, Public Records Office, including, documents from the Colonial Office, Board of Trade, and Treasurer's Office
Colonial Court Records
Chowan County Records including, Bonds, Minutes of the County Court of Pleas and Quarter Sessions, Estates, Wills, County Accounts, Orders and Decrees of the Court of Pleas and Quarter Sessions, Minutes of the Board of Magistrates, Miscellaneous Records, Miscellaneous Papers, Letters and Papers of James Norcom, Letters and Papers of Elisha Norfleet
Edenton Town Council Minutes, 1865—1960
Edenton Town Lot Book
English Records Calendar
Journals of the North Carolina General Assembly
Governors Papers—Tryon and Martin
Joseph Hewes Papers
James Iredell Papers
Charles Johnston Collection
Papers of James Parker, Liverpool Public Library (microfilm)
Thomas Pollock Papers
Papers of the Secretary of State
Journals of the Society for the Propagation of the Gospel (microfilm)
State Agency Collection, including, Treasurer and Comptroller's Papers and County Settlements with the State
United States Census Records

Miscellaneous Maps, Photographs, and Newspapers

Newspapers

Edenton Based:

Albemarle Bulletin
Albemarle Enquirer
Albemarle Intelligencer
Albemarle Observer
Albemarle Sentinel
American Banner
Chowan Herald

Eastern Courier
Edenton Clarion
Edenton Gazette
Encyclopedic Instructor
Fisherman and Farmer
State Gazette of N.C.

Non-Edenton newspapers include the *Virginia Gazette,* Williamsburg, Va. and various New Bern papers.

Primary Sources, Published

Asbury, Francis. Edited by Elmer Clark. *Journals and Letters of Francis Asbury.* London: Epworth Press, 1958.

Cappon, Lester and Duff, Stella. *Index to Virginia Gazette 1736–1780.* Williamsburg, Va.: Williamsburg Institute of Early American History and Culture, 1950.

Clark, Walter L., ed. *State Records of North Carolina.* 16 Vols. numbered XI–XXVI. Winston and Goldsboro: State of North Carolina, 1895–1906.

Craig, James. *Arts and Crafts in North Carolina 1699–1840.* Winston-Salem: Museum of Early Southern Decorative Arts, 1965.

Fouts, Raymond P. *Abstracts from the State Gazette of North Carolina.* Cocoa, Fl.: GenRec Books, 1984.

Fries, Adelaide, ed. *Records of the Moravians in North Carolina,* Vol. I: "Bishop Spangenberg's Diary." Raleigh, N.C.: North Carolina Historical Commission, 1922.

_____. *Abstracts of Newspapers of Edenton, Fayetteville, and Hillsborough, North Carolina 1785–1800.* Cocoa, Fl.: GenRec Books, 1984.

_____. *Vestry Minutes of St. Paul's Parish, Chowan County, North Carolina 1701–1776.* Cocoa, Fl.: GenRec Books, 1983.

Grimes, J. Bryan, ed. *Abstracts of North Carolina Wills.* Raleigh, N.C.: E.M. Uzzell, 1910.

_____. *North Carolina Wills and Inventories.* Raleigh, N.C.: Edwards and Broughton, 1912.

Hathaway J.R.B. *North Carolina Historical and Genealogical Register,* 3 Vols. Edenton, North Carolina: 1900–1903.

Haun, Weynette P., compiler. *Chowan County, North Carolina Court Minutes Pleas and Quarter Sessions,* 2 Vols.: 1730–1745; 1735–1738, 1746–1748. Durham, North Carolina: Haun, 1983 and 1984 respectively.

_____. *Old Albemarle County North Carolina Book of Land Warrents and Surveys 1681–1706.* Durham, North Carolina: Haun, 1984.

_____. *Old Albemarle County North Carolina Miscellaneous Records, 1678–ca. 1737.* Durham, N.C.: Haun, 1982.

Higginbotham, Don, ed. *Papers of James Iredell 1767–1783,* 2 Vols. Raleigh, N.C.: North Carolina Division of Archives and History, 1976.

Hoffman, Margaret M., compiler. *Chowan Precinct, North Carolina 1693–1723, Genealogical Abstracts of Deed Books.* Weldon, N.C.: Roanoke News Co., 1972.

_____. *Province of North Carolina Abstracts of Land Patents.* Weldon, North Carolina: Roanoke News Co., 1979.

Lee, Reverend Jesse. *Memoir of the Reverend Jesse Lee with extracts of his Journals.* Minton Thrift, editor. New York: N. Bangs and T. Mason for the Methodist Episcopal Church, 1823.

Lee, Leroy. *The Life and Times of the Reverend Jesse Lee.* Richmond, Va.: John Early for the Methodist Episcopal Church South, 1848.

Lemmon, Sarah, ed. *Pettigrew Papers 1665–1818.* Raleigh, N.C.: Division of Archives and History, 1971.

Parker, Matie Erma Edwards; Price, William S; and Cain, Robert J., editors. *The Colonial Records of North Carolina.* Second Series, 7 Vols. to date. Raleigh, N.C.: Division of Archives and History, 1964–1984.

Pilmore, Joseph. *Journal of Joseph Pilmore—Methodist Itinerant.* Frederick Maser and Howard T. Maag, editors. Philadelphia: Historical Society of the Philadelphia Annual Conference of the United Methodist Church, 1969 reprint.

Powell, William S., ed. *Correspondence and Papers of William Tryon,* 2 Vols. Raleigh, N.C.: Division of Archives and History, 1980-81.

Saunders, William L., ed. *Colonial Records of North Carolina,* 10 Vols. Raleigh, N.C.: State of North Carolina, 1886–1890.

Secondary Sources

Banks, William N. and Elizabeth Vann Moore. "History in Towns, Edenton, N.C." *Antiques,* June 1979.

Barber, Ira W., Jr. "The Ocean Borne Commerce of Port Roanoke 1771–1776." M.A. Thesis, UNC-CH, 1931.

Bishir, Catherine. "Black Builders in Antebellum N.C." *North Carolina Historical Review,* (NCHR), October 1984.

Boyce, W. Scott. *Economic and Social History of Chowan County 1880–1915.* New York: Columbia University Press, 1917.

Boyd, Julien. "County Court in Colonial N.C." M.A. Thesis, Duke University, Durham, North Carolina, 1926.

Bridenbaugh, Carl. *The Colonial Craftsman.* New York: New York University Press, 1950.

Burns, Robert, Project director. *One Hundred Courthouses, A Report on N. C. Judicial Facilities,* 2 Vols. Raleigh, N.C.: North Carolina State School of Design, 1978.

Cheeseman, Bruce S. "Historical Research Report: The Cupola House of Edenton, N.C." Raleigh, N.C.: Research Branch of Division of Archives and History, 1980.

Corbitt, David L. *Formation of N.C Counties 1663–1943.* Raleigh, N.C.: Division of Archives and History, 1943.

Cotton, William D. "North Carolina As Seen Through the Eyes of Travellers 1524–1729." M.A. Thesis, UNC-CH, 1949.

Crittenden, Charles C. and Don Lacy, ed. *Historical Records of North Carolina—County Records,* (Chowan Co., Vol. II, pp. 415–434). Raleigh, N.C.: North Carolina Historical Commission, 1938.

_____. "Means of Communication in North Carolina 1763–1789." *NCHR,* October 1931.

Dill, Alonzo Thomas, Jr. *Governor Tryon and His Palace.* Chapel Hill, N.C.: University of North Carolina Press, 1955.

_____. "Tryon Palace: Neglected Niche of North Carolina History." *NCHR,* April 1942.

_____. "Eighteenth Century New Bern." *NCHR,* July 1946.

Dillard, Richard. *A Brief History of Edenton and its Environs.* Elizabeth City, N.C.: The Independent, n.d.

_____. *The Civil War in Chowan County, North Carolina,* 1916.

_____. "St. Paul's Church and Its Associations." *North Carolina Booklet,* 1905.

_____. "Edenton, Rich in Colonial History." *Carolina Magazine,* June 1933.

Foss, Robert et al. *Archeological Investigations of the Edenton Snuff and Tobacco Manufacture.* Raleigh, N.C.: North Carolina Archeological Council and Archeology Branch of the Division of Archives and History, 1979.

Grissom, W. L. *History of Methodism in North Carolina from 1772 to the Present Time.* Nashville, TN.: Smith and Lamar, 1905.

Guess, William C. *County Government in Colonial North Carolina.* James Sprunt Studies in History and Political Science, Vols. 16–17. Chapel Hill, N.C.: University of North Carolina, 1911.

Holmes, George B. *History of St. Paul's Eposcopal Church in Edenton, North Carolina- together with a guide to the Churchyard Epitaphs.* Edenton, N.C.: St. Pauls's Church, 1964.

Isham, Norman Morrison. *Glossary of Colonial Architectural Terms with Bibliography of Books 1880–1930 and The Dating of Old Houses.* Watkins Glen, N.Y.: American Life Federation, 1968.

Johnson, Francis and Thomas Waterman. *Early Architecture of North Carolina.* Chapel Hill, N.C.: University of North Carolina Press, 1941.

Lane, Mills. *Architecture of the Old South.* Savannah, Ga.: Beehive Press, 1985.

Lefler, H.T., ed. *North Carolina History told by Contemporaries.* Chapel Hill, N.C.: University of North Carolina Press, 1934.

Lefler, H.T. and Albert Newsome. *North Carolina–The History of a Southern State.* Third Edition. Chapel Hill, N.C.: University of North Carolina Press, 1973.

Lefler, H.T. and William S. Powell. *Colonial North Carolina–A History.* New York: Charles Scribners and Sons, 1973.

Lemmon, Sarah McCulloh. *Parson Pettigrew of the Old Church 1744–1807.* James Sprunt Studies in History and Political Science, Vol. 52. Chapel Hill, N.C.: University of North Carolina, 1970.

Loundsbury, Carl. "Order in the Court–Recommendations for the Restoration of the James City County/Williamsburg Courthouse." Williamsburg, Va.: Archeological Research Department, Colonial Williamsburg, October 1985.

McCain, Paul. *The County Government in N.C Before 1750.* Durham, N.C.: Duke University Press, 1954.

McKee, Harley J. *Introduction to Early American Masonry.* Published for the National Trust for Historic Preservation and Columbia University, 1973.

McRee, Griffith S. *Life and Correspondence of James Iredell.* 2 Vols. New York: Appleton and Co., 1857–58.

Marley, Branson. "Minutes of the General Court of Albemarle, 1684." *NCHR,* January 1942.

Martin, Michael G. "Joseph Hewes 'Reluctant Revolutionary': A Study of a North Carolina Whig and the War for American Independence." M.A. Thesis, UNC-CH, 1969.

Matheson, Elizabeth. *Edenton, Portrait in Words and Pictures*. Edenton, N.C.: Edenton Historical Commission, 1984.

Merrens, Harry Roy. *Colonial North Carolina in the Eighteenth Century*. Chapel Hill, N.C.: University of North Carolina Press, 1964.

Millar, John Fitzhugh. *Architects of the American Colonies*. Barre, MA.: Barre, 1968.

Morrison, Hugh. *Early American Architecture*. New York: Oxford University Press, 1952.

Nash, F. "Borough Towns of North Carolina." *North Carolina Booklet*, 1906.

North Carolina Baptist Papers. "The Organization and Building of the Edenton Baptist Church." *The Wake Forest Student*, Vol. xxvi #1, September 1906.

Olton, Charles. *Artisans for Independence*. Syracuse, N.Y.: Syracuse University Press, 1975.

Pare, Richard, ed. *Courthouse: A Photographic Document*. New York: Horizon Press, 1978.

Parramore, Thomas C. *Cradle of the Colony: The History of Chowan County and Edenton, N.C.* Edenton, N.C.: Edenton Chamber of Commerce, 1967.

Paschal, George Washington. *History of North Carolina's Baptists 1663–1803*. Raleigh, N.C.: General Board of the North Carolina Baptist State Convention, 1930.

_____. *History of Printing in North Carolina*. Raleigh, N.C.: Edward and Broughton Co., 1946.

Paschal, Herbert R. "Proprietary North Carolina: A Study in Colonial Government." Ph.D. Dissertation, UNC-CH, 1961.

Peatross, C. Ford. *William Nichols, Architect of the Old South*. University, Alabama: University of Alabama Art Gallery, 1979.

Pierson, William H., Jr. *American Buildings and Their Architects: The Colonial and Neo Colonial Styles*. New York: Doubleday and Co. Inc., 1970.

Powell, Diana. "Artisans in the Colonial South, Chowan County 1714–1776." M.A. Thesis, UNC-CH, 1982.

Powell, William S. *Bibliography of North Carolina Counties*. Raleigh, N.C.: Division of Archives and History, 1952.

Raper, Charles Lee. *North Carolina, A Study in English Colonial Government*. New York: Macmillan, 1904.

Sharpe, Bill. *A New Geography of North Carolina*. 4 Vols. Raleigh, N.C.: Sharpe Publishing Co., 1956–65.

Smith, Helen B. and Elizabeth Vann Moore. "John Mare: A Composite Portrait." NCHR, 1967.

Vaughn, F. E. *The Albemarle Section of North Carolina Traversed by the Norfolk Southern Railroad*. Elizabeth City, N.C., 1884.

Warren, Mary Alethea. *Historic Buildings of Edenton, N.C.* Edenton, N.C., (1927?)

Wilborn, Elizabeth, researcher. "Edenton, North Carolina: An Historical Sketch and Pictorial Essay." *Southern Antiques and Interiors*, Vol. #3. (Fall 1972). Raleigh, N.C.: Division of Historical Sites and Museums, North Carolina Office of Archives and History.

Travel and Descriptions

Byrd, William. *Histories of the Dividing Line Betwixt Virginia and North Carolina.* William K. Boyd, ed. Raleigh, N.C.: North Carolina Historical Commission, 1929.

Brickell, John. *Natural History of North Carolina.* Thomas Parramore, introduction. Reprint of 1737 edition. Murfreesboro, N.C.: Johnson Publishing Co., 1968.

Finlay, Hugh. *Journal Kept by Hugh Finlay Surveyor of the Post Roads on the Continent of North America...13 September 1773—26 June 1774.* F.H. Norton, 1867. (Available on microfilm, UNC-CH, North Carolina Collection.)

Johnson, Hugh Buckner. "Ebenezer Hazard's Journal." *NCHR,* 1959.

Lawson, John. *A New Voyage to Carolina.* Reprint of 1726 edition. Chapel Hill, N.C.: University of North Carolina Press, 1967.

Salley, Alexander S., Jr., ed. *Narratives of Early Carolina 1650—1708.* New York: Charles Scribners, 1911.

Schopf, Johan David. *Travels in the Confederation.* Alfred Morrison, trans. Philadelphia, PA.: William J. Campbell, 1911.

Strother, David Hunter. *The Old South Illustrated.* (from articles appearing in Harpers Monthly 1853—1858). Chapel Hill, N.C.: University of North Carolina Press, 1959.

Warren, Edward. *A Doctor's Experience in Three Continents.* Baltimore, MD.: Cushings and Bailey, 1885.

Wright, Louis B. and Marion Tinling, editors. *Quebec to Carolina 1785-86 Being the Observations of Robert Hunter Jr. Young Merchant of London.* San Marino, CA.: Huntington Library, 1943.

ML